ONCE A LITTLE FROG IN THE WELL

My Joseon Memoirs

Sue Sackrider

"A Frog in the Well" 우물 안에 개구리 *is an old Korean proverb, based on a fable by Zhuāng Zǐ about a frog and a sea turtle. It is used to describe a sheltered and close-minded individual who cannot or refuses to see the big picture. As the famous story goes, there was once a frog who lived in a small well. With all the fresh water to drink and swim in, mud to play with, and lots of insects to eat, he felt like the king of the world and was very happy. One day he had a visitor, a turtle from the East Sea. He invited the turtle over to come inside his well and look at the magnificent world he was living in. The turtle tried going inside through the narrow opening of the well but got stuck. After much trying, he finally gave up. Realizing how small the well was, he started telling the frog about the great East Sea. He said, "The size of the East Sea is beyond your wildest imagination. Even a distance of a thousand miles cannot give you an idea of the sea's width; even the height of a thousand feet cannot give you an idea of its depth. In the time of King Da Yu, there were floods nine years out of ten, but the waters in the sea did not increase. During the time of King Tang, there were droughts seven years out of eight, but the waters in the sea did not decrease. After all, the sea does not change with the passage of time, and its level does not rise or fall according to the amount of rain that falls. Living in the East Sea is the greatest happiness." Hearing these words, the frog felt very insignificant and realized how limited his perspective was.*

I've written these memoirs to remind me that I was once like this little frog in a well, but when a "sea turtle" came into my life (a metaphor for my husband Bill) I was freed from my limited perspective to experience an entirely new world.

Table of Contents

Introduction

My main motivation for writing this book is to preserve my family's history and to organize the memories I have as a legacy for them. Despite having had many extraordinary experiences in my life, I realize I've forgotten some of them. Yet I still clearly remember certain events, as if seeing photographs in my head.

It may be hard to understand what life was like in Korea as I grew up compared to the way things are now. I was born on May 22, 1944, during World War II, which ended over a year later on September 2, 1945. I was six years old when the Korean War started in 1950, a battle which lasted another three years. Although I was too young to properly comprehend what was happening at the time, many of my recollections from that period are still distinct. In our village, there was a lot of fear and panic, and many families were harmed.

My dad, mother, younger brother Seok-Gu, and I resided in my father's Yi family house along with my paternal grandparents, aunts, and uncles. The family-owned a large amount of flat land filled with rice paddies, most of which my father eventually lost due to his gambling. During war time the young men fled to hide, leaving only the elderly and mothers with young children in most homes. My father was in hiding too, showing up late at night for a short time but gone by early morning. I recall people continually searching the sky and listening for warplanes. I remember running for cover into our homemade underground shelter or other temporary hiding places.

Since we lived in the countryside, we didn't have easy access to news - there was no newspaper, radio, or TV. Most of our information came by word of mouth through neighbors and village leaders. Once in a while, my grandma would hear things from her church congregation, who were more educated and knowledgeable than most of the villagers. Still, we were not sure if the information was true or reliable. It was very confusing and hard to know who our enemy was, and who wasn't a threat. People fought over ideology and split into two camps. One thing I knew for sure from listening to their conversations was that our family did not like the Communists. They loved our president, Syngman Rhee, who was the first president of South Korea, because he was educated in an American university. He was well-known in the Christian community and considered a very smart man. My family liked him because they believed he was a good Christian man, and they thought he would make the country better.

Most of the conflict and bombing was closer to the city of Seoul, where many people were killed. Some families tried to avoid the dangers of war by escaping to the countryside. The train from Seoul passed through the city once or twice a day, and I heard that during the war, it was packed with people sitting on top or hanging onto the side doors. Even though we were about

35-40 minutes walking distance from the train station, many of the houses in our village, including ours took in these strange people from Seoul. They would only stay a few days, often sleeping outside on the patio before continuing their journey, but then someone new would come to take their place. I saw my grandma feed them nourishing food, but we still had plenty of beans, dried greens, potatoes, and different grains in our food pantry. I don't remember being hungry at my grandparents' house, but later when my father moved us out of his family's home we often didn't have enough food.

These are the details I remember about the Korean War. Meanwhile, with chaos raging all around me, my childhood memories are even more scarred because of an abusive home life. My father was an alcoholic with a terrible gambling addiction, and he frequently took out his anger on his family. His own parents were afraid of him, after having doted on him as an only child for nearly ten years before his first brother was born. Although he was charming and nice to people outside the family, at home my father ruled the household like a tyrannical dictator. Whenever he came around, everyone in the family started to whisper, on alert as if in a state of emergency.

Little did I know at the time, but the conversion of his mother, my cherished grandma, to Christianity around 1948 was the biggest blessing. This helped lay the groundwork for my brighter future. My father's two brothers and two sisters also became Christians, but my father was never interested. My father's youngest brother, Uncle Jong-Su, later gave me the opportunity to earn a living and become independent when I was 17 years old.

I am so grateful that God gave me a better life in America with my husband Bill and that his family also welcomed not only me but my parents and siblings. Their support helped us overcome the many challenges of immigrant life and assimilation. Within a few years of arriving in this country, I was able to bring my mother, father, four brothers, and sister from Korea. After 52 years of marriage, Bill and I have been blessed with three wonderful daughters, five grandsons, and one granddaughter. God has been with me through my entire life, and he still gives me strength in all circumstances. It is my hope and prayer for this book to help my daughters and grandchildren, as well as my brothers and sister, nieces, and nephews to understand my history and theirs.

Chapter 1
A Brief History of Korea

Korea is a peninsula located in the easternmost part of the Asian continent between China and Japan. In the early 1900s, the countries of Japan, Russia, and China all fought for control over Korea because of its resources and strategic location - access to water made the country an important trading hub. From 1904-1905, the Empire of Russia and the Empire of Japan were engaged in the Russo-Japanese War, with Japan as the victor, occupying Korea in 1905 and annexing our country in 1910. Every family that resided in Korea, including mine, was significantly impacted by 20th-century events. Even though South Korea has grown into one of the important and influential nations in the world today, past struggles and sacrifices remain vivid for many Koreans, passed down through generations. The trauma of war, separation from loved ones, and the quest for peace and reunification continue to shape Korean society and national identity.

From the start of the oppressive Japanese occupation, Koreans battled to preserve their culture. As a means of assimilating Koreans into their nation, the Japanese closed Korean schools and constructed their own institutions in our country. Korean history and the Korean language were forbidden in these schools, which only taught the Japanese language. Many historical records were destroyed. Koreans were forced to adopt Japanese names and to learn Japanese as a second language. The right to assemble, associate, publish, and speak freely were among the many liberties that were taken away.

The Japanese policy was to industrialize Korea. A new monetary system was established, and national transportation and communication networks were constructed. Buildings were taken over by the Japanese government and military, and Korean-owned companies were also turned over to the Japanese government. New firms that benefited the Japanese were launched, while Korean business startups were not permitted. For Korean people, finding work was challenging.

Farmers were also required to record the acreage and size of their land. Their land would be taken away from them if they refused. Those who were permitted to keep their land were required to give Japan a large portion of their crops. Village agriculture and woodlands were seized by the Japanese, and starvation started to threaten the Korean population. Some escaped into the woods, where it was challenging to survive. Others left the country and moved to Manchuria or Japan in search of opportunity, where they were subjected to injustice and persecution merely because they were Korean. Throughout the entire period of Japanese colonization, Koreans attempted to reclaim power through uprisings and revolts, but none were successful.

World War II started in 1939 when the Allied Powers, led by Great Britain, the United States, and the Soviet Union, resisted the Axis powers made up of Germany, Italy, and Japan. Korean men were forced to join Japan's military or work in industries to support war efforts, frequently in hazardous, slave-like conditions. Thousands of Korean girls and women were abducted by Japanese forces and used as "comfort women" to perform sex acts for the soldiers. When nuclear bombs decimated the cities of Hiroshima and Nagasaki, Japan realized that the end of the war was imminent. In 1945, the Allies declared victory, and Japan retreated. Despite this good news and Korea achieving independence, our nation had to start all over after the ravages of war.

When the war ended, the United States and the Soviet Union decided to divide the Korean Peninsula into two occupation zones at the 38th parallel, creating North Korea and South Korea. The Soviets took charge of the North, while the U.S. supported the South which became a Republic. South Korea made an effort to establish democracy after being ruled by Japan for so long.

The 38th Parallel divides the Korean peninsula. Photo from Wikimedia Commons

The Democratic People's Republic of Korea, also known as North Korea, founded its capital city in Pyongyang. At the same time, the Republic of Korea (South Korea) built its capital city in Seoul in August 1948. The ROK (Republic of Korea) Army was founded by South Korean President Syngman Rhee, and the KPA (Korean People's Army) was created by North Korea's leader Kim Il Sung. Sadly, the independence of our nation was short-lived. North Korean troops invaded South Korea by crossing the 38th parallel on June 25, 1950. The ROK army was forced to battle for its life. The South Korean army lacked the necessary firepower and supplies, and the soldiers lacked experience in extensive warfare. They couldn't compete with the North Korean military, which Russia had equipped and trained. The Korean War began at this point. During this conflict, soldiers from the United States and the UN fought alongside South Korean forces while Russia and China supported the North Koreans. The destruction of enterprises and the ensuing widespread poverty among the populace made this a particularly tragic period for Korea. Three million Koreans were dead, injured, or missing by the time the war concluded in 1953.

Korean refugee children, Korean War, 1951. Image courtesy Wikimedia Commons

The Demilitarized Zone (DMZ) is a region along the 38th parallel that was established after the conflict. A third of the total population of the two Korean states, containing about 10 million South Korean families with family or ancestors in North Korea, were prevented from crossing the demilitarized zone (DMZ).

After the war, Koreans endured numerous hardships and widespread poverty as they struggled to survive. The new government system caused a lot of confusion and many of the people were uneducated. Families that had been split up suffered unspeakable anguish. Hopelessness spread like a sickness. So much of our old culture was lost. Some would contend that Korea and its people are still attempting to define their actual identity generations later. It's hard to imagine how difficult life must have been for Koreans, with one conflict after another after suffering 500 years under Joseon rule (more on this later).

Chapter 2
Mom and Dad

My Mom's Family

My mother's name was Sun-Hyun Yu (유순현) (1922-2019). Her family lived in Chungyang County, which is part of Chungnam Province in South Korea. Her mother had the surname Myong, and her father had the surname Yu (유). My mother had three siblings - two brothers and one sister. Sung-Hyun (성현) was the eldest son, followed by my mother, then her brother Young-Hyun (영현), and her younger sister Emo. (The term Emo refers to aunt. I don't remember her real name because in Korean tradition, children do not address adults by name, especially if they are married women. Therefore, young kids usually do not know the names of people older than them.) Emo arrived ten years after my mother's birth.

16

My mother's family were merchants and relatively well-off. They made most of their money by selling products at the market. The city had a market every five days, when people from surrounding towns and villages would shop for items they needed. The Yu's sold clothing, shoes, bags, sewing machines, medicines, and creams for women among many other items. Mom's brother Young-Hyun was good at predicting the latest trends and determining which products would be the most profitable. He owned a sewing machine and used it to open a custom leather shoe store that was increasingly popular for people who could afford it. Much of what was sold came from or was influenced by Japan, because most people considered products from Japan as well-made. Under Japan's colonial rule, the Korean people lived with much suffering, but they had no choice except to work with Japan in order to survive.

I recall my mother saying that her life was mostly content and calm in her childhood home. They supported and respected each other, and didn't worry about having enough food to eat, even when the rest of the country's circumstances were tough.

My Dad's Family

My father's name was Jong-Man Yi (이종만) (1917-1997). Dad was the oldest of five children, with two younger brothers - Jong-Seok (종석) and Jong-Su - (종수) and two younger sisters - Jong-Ye (종애) and Jong-Lim (종림). Jun-Ju Yi was his father's family name. They were descendants of the Yi Dynasty (1392-1919), also known as the Joseon Dynasty. It was Korea's final and longest-lasting imperial dynasty, as well as the highest class during the 500 years before Japan took over the country. His mother's surname was Park.

My great, great grandfather was a somewhat wealthy man who received a lot of land from his parents. My great grandfather left the farm to my grandfather, who was the eldest son in the Yi family. It included a rice paddy (a flooded land used for rice cultivation) that was eventually partitioned into three portions, one for each son.

In traditional Korean culture, the eldest son has special privileges and obligations, based on Confucian ideals. My father received the most land, but he also had the specific responsibility to help his parents during their lifetime. The eldest son was expected to live in the family home, while the younger siblings had to make their own living arrangements. After his parents died, my dad should have been the head of the family, maintaining the Confucious ancestor worship rituals and ceremonial services every holiday, such as remembering the day of one's parents' death. There were five generations who lived in that house - I was the last generation to live in the family Yi home.

Dad's Early Life

Both of my grandparents struck me as kind-hearted and empathetic. Even though I was a girl, I had a special bond because I was their first surviving grandchild. My mom had already lost a son at one year old before I was born. I'm sure they wished I was a boy too, but they never showed that to me. However, because of my father's actions, there was a lot of stress in our household. My father seemed to be the source of most of our family's troubles. It's still difficult for me to talk about my father because it brings up so many painful memories.

Little children are lavished with care and pampered in traditional Korean culture. Parents teach their children to be reliant, obedient, and cooperative. As I already stated, my father was the oldest child. Jong-Seok, his younger brother, was born when he was ten years old. My grandmother claimed that my father was spoiled by everyone because he had been the only child for so long. She told me that while she was pregnant with my father, she had a dream in which a big dragon appeared from the river in front of our house and flew straight up to heaven. She took this as a good omen, and she predicted that her child would be particularly exceptional. (This was before she converted to Christianity).

My father went to a traditional private school where he learned Chinese characters and philosophy. My grandparents believed this was important because they thought my father, as the eldest, would take over the family responsibilities in accordance with Confucious customs. My father, however, wanted to continue his studies at a Korean and Japanese institution. My grandparents would not allow this since it was during the Japanese invasion, when Korean people had to learn and speak Japanese, as well as change their names and Korean history in the process.

According to my grandmother, my father was a smart boy, and she couldn't understand why he rebelled and turned into an unruly son who associated with drunkards, loafers, and gamblers. Although I thought there was no excuse for my father's behavior, it should be noted that his generation faced many challenges. Based on stories my grandmother told me, I believe the turmoil in our country contributed to much of his bitterness, drinking, and gambling. I would often hear my father yelling at my grandparents and blaming them for his failures in life. One excuse he often used was that they did not allow him to go to a modern school like his younger siblings. Even though I was just a kid, I thought it was ridiculous for him to blame them since many others were in similar situations but did not act like my father.

Chapter 3
The Korean War 1950-1953

After World War II, the Korean peninsula was divided into two occupation zones that were intended to be temporary. A unified state was never given back to the newly independent Korean people. Instead, the Korean War broke out between the Soviet and Chinese-backed North, and the United States and United Nations-backed South.

Hiding from Communists

Before the war, everyone in our village seemed to get along. But as a result of the war, people were hesitant to trust each other. A person might call someone a friend one day, but the next day be unsure about their alliances. Many South Korean men were taken by the communist North Korean and Chinese soldiers during the war. Some were imprisoned in North Korean POW (prisoner of war) camps and were never released. As a result, most of the adult males, including my father and uncles, hid with relatives or in the distant mountains to evade capture.

During this time, my mom's older brother Sung-Hyun bought an agricultural waste processing facility. Unfortunately, at the start of the Korean war when he was just 40 years old, he died of appendicitis. He left behind a wife and a little boy so his younger brother Young-Hyun took over the mill. Soon after, Young-Hyun was injured in a mill accident and needed assistance, so he invited Dad to work there. My father was not interested, but he agreed because he needed money and a safe haven from the Communists.

Mom's family lived about 50 miles south of us. We didn't visit often because it took us an entire day to get there by bus and on foot. I was six and Seok-Gu was four when Dad decided to go to the mill. He sent Mom and Seok-Gu there first, then Dad and I followed a week later. We rode on Dad's bike much of the way. Somewhere along the route he left me at the home of distant relatives I had never seen before - two elderly ladies who looked like sisters. Dad dropped me off and immediately left, and said he would return for me. I expected him to be gone for a couple hours, but he was gone for a few days. The ladies gave me a little porridge but said nothing, and I was too afraid to ask any questions. Terrified, I wondered if he would ever come back and take me to my mother. Later, I discovered he was being chased by strangers, so he had to quickly find a hiding place. He finally returned with no explanation and just said, "let's go," then strapped me to the back of his bike. I had no idea at the time that he had chosen a route across the mountains without roads for part of the way. This was to avoid detection, because no one could trust anyone at that time. We traveled mostly at night and slept on the ground during the day. I remember drinking water from small rushing creeks and eating sweet potatoes. We had multiple mishaps on the bike that left us bloodied and injured. I felt hopeless as I watched Dad struggle with me on the bike, while falling down and cursing to himself. He appeared desperate. I walked behind him quietly much of the time as he pushed the bike. I'm not sure how long it took us to reach our destination, but it seemed like a week or more.

We lived with Uncle Young-Hyun for about three months before Dad decided that the work was below him. He was miserable the entire time, and let us all know it. Mom, Seok-Gu, and I stayed for another three months or so before returning home to rejoin my father's family.

When the fighting stopped in 1953, we felt we could resume normal life. However, the Korean War never formally ended and is still unresolved today. There were numerous heartbreaking stories involving divided families and loved ones. Despite the fact that the land was extremely valuable, there were no prospects of work. The majority of South Koreans remained impoverished. Almost everything was destroyed in Seoul during the conflict. Many places needed to be rebuilt, but families living in cities had a considerably more difficult time because most of the combat took place in the big centers.

With the devastation from the war, people of all ages did almost anything to survive. The cities were full of homeless people and orphans. Many young girls had to quit school to work in factories for very little money to try to support their families. The postwar Korean government seemed overwhelmed; they didn't know where to start rebuilding the country's infrastructure. Those years were very difficult and sad times in Korea when I was growing up.

While our country was in disarray, my father's behavior continued to cause havoc in our household.

Chapter 4
Village Life 1944-1961

Our family lived in Yongdong-Ri, a village located near a small city called Sapgyo-Eup in the county of Yesan-gun, about 46 miles northwest of Daejeon. My memory of our village was a lovely, lush green countryside. It was built around a river in the Gayasahn Mountains foothills. We had to cross a wooden bridge to go to the other side of the river, where there were acres of rice paddies so enormous that we couldn't see the city in the distance. Farmers from our village and the neighboring villages farmed together in this area. We had no electricity in our village, although the adults hoped we would be able to get electric power soon so we could have light. Once they had electricity, they would be able to start using it in many ways, but at the time we didn't have electric appliances or equipment.

In order to go to the city, we had to walk for an hour. At the city markets, people sold clothing, shoes, vegetables, rabbits, chickens, and every kind of farm animal that you could imagine. There were butcher shops and one modern doctor's office in our little town, as well as an acupuncture or herbal doctor's office for locals who could afford it. There was also an elementary school, a Catholic church, a Methodist church, and an Evangelical Holiness Church, which is a denomination similar to Methodist.

Our home was a hanok, a traditional Korean house first designed in the 14th century during the Yi Dynasty. Five generations of the Yi family lived in this old house. Korean architecture took into account the house's location in relation to its surroundings. According to the baesanimsu or Feng Shui principle, an ideal house should have a mountain in the back and a river in front. Hanoks were designed in a square with a courtyard in the center to better retain heat in Korea's frigid northern areas. Hanoks in the south were more open and L-shaped. Even now, I think when Korean houses are built, especially in the country, they use this traditional style.

Our house was the biggest home in the center of our small village. It was shaped like a square with an upper and lower level and a courtyard. To get to the courtyard, we had to pass through a large gate known as a da-mon that looped around the house to keep strangers out. The walls were made of clay bricks and wood, while the flooring was a mixture of stone, clay, and wood. Because rice grass was plentiful during harvest, it was used for roofing material, to make bags to hold grain, and even for constructing old-fashioned shoes. Farmers twisted and braided rice straw during the winter months to help one another reinforce their roofs when necessary. However, I never saw my dad, uncles, or grandpa do any kind of farm labor.

In traditional Korean culture, men and women frequently did things separately during the day, but by dinner the entire family was back together. In our house, the largest room was on the ground floor and had two doors that led outside and one door that led inside to a little kitchen. The large room was known as the Sarang bang, which translates as "male guest room." Men gathered here to hold meetings, entertain guests and sleep. On one side, there was a vast space for storing grain and other kinds of food, much like a large pantry. On the opposite side, there were smaller storage facilities and a small kitchen next to the Sarang bang. Our primary kitchen was located on the upper level next to the main living room and the patio which was called maru or dachung. We had to build fires to be able to cook, and the fire's smoke was routed through the floors by chimneys to keep the house warm and heat the entire home. The three upper-level bedrooms were generally occupied by women, grandparents, and children.

We were about a half mile uphill from a large clear sandy river filled with sand and pebbles. At dawn, we watched the water levels change depending on how much it had rained. The adults wore white most of the time while children wore plain, simple clothing and black rubber shoes. From middle school, girls commonly wore a black skirt and white top uniform, right up until they were in high school. Boys wore all black. (The kids like me who couldn't go to school felt ashamed because they weren't able to wear this uniform. This added to my own inferiority complex in my young life.) Women washed laundry with homemade soap, while pounding and rubbing their garments on the river rocks. During the warm months, as women washed their family's clothes, the children would go swimming and catch little fish, crawdads, and snails in the shallow areas. Everyone would bathe in the river in the evenings. Men and boys went first, followed by the women and girls. As a child, I recall how much fun we had, although my father didn't participate since he was almost always gone.

I also recall how my brother Seok-Gu and I were happy whenever Dad was away. I have good memories from this time period when I was about five through nine. But then we left the family home with my father and didn't come back until I was 14. By then, a lot of things had changed in the village. A new concrete dam had been constructed to help direct water to the rice paddies, and the man-made addition dramatically changed the natural landscape. The beautiful river with sand and pebbles wasn't there anymore, and not much was left of the lush green countryside. I was very sad that the life I remembered was gone.

In those days, we would eat what we could grow in our garden, like potatoes, cabbage, and radishes along with many other vegetables. We also knew which wild edible plants would be growing each spring season that we could gather. Food was very important for every household. Our country was in such chaos, and there was still a shortage of food, with hungry people everywhere. People living in the cities were much worse off than those in the countryside like us. We also were not close to the north where most of the fighting had happened. Our main crop was rice, but we also grew barley, beans, and other grains. Rice was the most important crop since it was viewed as a luxury and the most profitable. As a result, many farmers were unable to personally eat the rice they grew but were forced to sell it.

Back then, everyone made their own tofu, bean sprouts, miso, soy sauce, hot sauce, and kimchi which is a traditional Korean dish. (Today nearly everyone buys these foods from grocery stores. There are also many kimchi and tofu factories.) Families had to have these ingredients as they were key to every meal. (We still have to have these same ingredients to cook most Korean dishes today.) Kimchi is the most important food next to rice for the Korean people. No one used a recipe but instead they made kimchi with whatever vegetables they already had in the house. Some of those old traditional methods still work for the modern Korean kitchens today, and people can make many different delicious kimchi dishes. The original kimchi was made by combining Napa cabbage and radishes, mixed with green onions, garlic, salt, hot pepper powder, and fish sauce. It can be made mild or spicy. Around the end of October, every house made winter kimchi. It was a big family event, and men helped place the winter kimchi in large pots that were buried in pots in the earth to keep them from freezing. Families would remove a small amount of kimchi from the big jars as needed during the winter months. (This is the traditional method of keeping kimchi. It's not necessary anymore because today nearly everyone has a kimchi refrigerator.)

Our mother often made kimchi soup and homemade miso soup with vegetables, occasionally with chicken. We ate chicken, eggs, and pork a few times a year, but beef much less because it was too expensive. Only a few people were able to raise cows, pigs, chickens, or goats, keeping them in a little shed next to their house. My favorite meal was rice with some vegetables and tofu. I also enjoyed rare treats of sticky rice and dumplings.

Because our house was in the center of the village and had a large yard with a communal spring well in the corner, children and adults gathered here. On most hot and humid summer evenings, people would bring their straw mats to sit in our yard. After a long day of hard work they looked forward to the evening. Men and women gathered in separate groups, and the men would build a fire with as much smoke as possible to chase away the mosquitos, while the children laid on mats attempting to count what seemed like a million stars in the black sky. Everyone enjoyed these sociable evenings.

Whenever I think about those times, a couple things remain in my memory. First, the bright beautiful stars in the black sky were an awesome sight. I still often look for stars on a dark night and it is one of my favorite things to do. My second memory is of a storyteller who we called Ajuma. Usually someone would tell stories and funny jokes, as well as share news from neighboring villages or the city. Ajuma was a very special and interesting lady who was our distant relative. She was a widow in her late 40s, who lived with her married son and his wife. All the village children loved her and named her Song Ajuma. Song was her last name and Ajuma means Aunt. Song Ajuma also loved us, and she usually came to sit with us in the children's area. I remember her stories could be funny, sad, happy, or very scary. Song Ajuma was naturally a very funny person; just looking at her face made us laugh. We'd ask her all kinds of questions, and she always answered as best she could. When a few of us girls first heard about menstruation and how babies came out of their mothers' wombs, we were so shaken. We were around 8 to 10 years old. Some girls thought she was lying or just crazy. The next day we decided to ask an older girl who was 14 years old, and she just nodded yes. Afterwards, whenever we had a question, we'd ask Song Ajuma.

Every year, Koreans celebrate different holidays based on the lunar calendar. We would make delicacies with rice cakes, and occasionally soup with meat. The Harvest Moon Festival (Chuseok) took place on the 15th day of the eighth month, normally in September, and children were treated to fun games. We also looked forward to the New Year (Seollal), which was the first day of the Korean lunar calendar. Most people ate the traditional rice cake dumpling soup in the morning. The girls would usually wear a traditional yellow top and a red long skirt. The boys would wear light blue pants and white tops with gray vests. Children were expected to bow down to the elders in their family. When possible, everyone gave them some money with a blessing.

Chapter 5
Dad's First Wife 1938

When my father was twenty years old, my grandmother picked a nice girl for him to marry, but he did not treat her well. It was normal for Korean parents to arrange marriages for their children, and my grandmother believed that once he was married, his behavior would change. He stayed at home with his wife for a few weeks before returning to his troubled friends. He would manipulate and use Grandma to obtain gambling money. Dad only came home when he was completely broke. This lasted for about two years while the girl waited for him to change. Her parents finally came to get her and told my grandmother it was not going to work out, and they brought their daughter back home. She eventually divorced my father, and my grandmother later learned that she had remarried. Grandma told me all this when I was a little older. I said good for her!

Within a few years of my dad's divorce, my grandmother made every effort to convince her eldest son to take over the Yi family as tradition dictated. Grandma was desperate to find him a new and proper wife again. She was still hopeful that her son would be happy at home and quit his self-destructive lifestyle. Grandma went through a lot of haggling and quarreling with my father, but by that time he was an addicted gambler and drunkard who didn't care about anything. Getting married again was not important to him, and the only thing he seemed to want was his parents' money for gambling. My grandpa was very weak emotionally, and he could not handle his son's uncontrollable behavior, so he stayed out of all family matters including finances. Grandma had to take over all family decisions. I am sure she realized she had to be the strong person in the house. Grandma somehow tracked down my mother's parents and arranged for my mom and my dad to marry. At the time, my mother was 19, and a matchmaker told my grandma that my mom's parents were looking for an older man who already had marital experience. It doesn't make sense to me now, but for some reason they thought he would be a better husband simply because he was older and had more experience in life. My father was 24 when they got married.

My parents never met or spoke to each other before their wedding - this was one of the many nonsensical old Joseon Korean customs that were adhered to for a long time. In keeping with tradition, our family resided with my father's parents in the house that had been in their family for many generations. It was uncommon for women to read at the time, but both my mother and father could read. Unfortunately, this skill did not appear to benefit our lives. In retrospect, I believe my parents' marriage was doomed from the start, and my mother could never have predicted how her life would change after she got married.

My father's siblings, including his younger sister (Jong-Lim) who was only 6 years older than me, also lived in the family home until they married. Jong-Ye, my oldest aunt, got married when she was very young, around 14 or 15. This was because during the Japanese occupation, my grandmother was concerned that her daughter might be seized by the Japanese imperialists. At that time military men took Korean women by force as comfort women or sex workers. So I don't have many memories of my older aunt as she left home when I was young.

Mom had 13 children over 22 years, although most were stillborn or died while they were young. During that era, almost all babies in the country were born at home with the help of their grandmothers or a midwife. Only six of my parents' children lived to adulthood. My parents named me Chong-Hee when I was born on May 22, 1944. (For some reason when I was six years old, my father legally changed my name to Chong-Su, but no one knew until I entered school at the age of seven. We think it's because he thought that my new name had more luck, but all my family and friends still refer to me as Chong-Hee).

My surviving siblings include my brother Seok-Gu born in 1946, brother Heung-Gu born in 1954, brother Jeong-Gu born in 1957, brother Tae-Gu born in 1959 and finally my sister Song-Hee born in 1964. My sister is twenty years younger than me and was born three years after I moved out of our home, so I didn't look after her as I did with my brothers.

Mom's childhood was similar to my father's in certain ways, but they were also quite different. Mom had a carefree, cheerful childhood. Her family had few issues, and her father was a caring and reliable provider. As the eldest daughter of four children, my mother was not required to do much housework, thus she had little experience with household chores. Typically, girls her age learned sewing, embroidery, and cooking, but my mother was not skilled in these areas and had no desire to learn. Instead, she wanted to get her chores over with quickly so she could spend more time outside playing with her friends, since she enjoyed being a tomboy.

After marrying my mother, Dad would strongly chastise my mom since his own mother and sisters were excellent cooks. Grandma would try to encourage and carefully teach my mother because she believed that if Mom mastered these skills, my father would calm down at home. In hindsight, even if my mother had these abilities, I don't believe it would have made much difference in my father's behavior. My mother also made no attempt to learn them because she knew my father's history and quickly understood that he would not change.

In the villages around us there were many men, including my dad, who seemed like professional gamblers. They gambled as if it was their job, doing no physical work - only drinking, gambling, fighting, womanizing, and making trouble. I can still remember the faces and the names of my dad's friends and gang leaders, Tacjul Im and Geyme Kim. I'm sure they've been dead for a long time. They were about the same age as my dad. I hated these drunk men and gamblers, especially since I encountered them many times when I had to go drag my father home or break up fights after their gambling. Unfortunately, these men had more free time when the rice harvest was over. This is when the farmers would sell and buy property and organize their finances. Rice was the same as money for most of the farmers. When the long winters began, Dad would sell some of his share of the rice paddies, and then he would abandon our family for months at a time. Nobody knew where he was or what he was doing when he was gone, nor did we ever ask him questions when he finally returned. We sometimes overheard what he told our neighbors. Once he said he bought large quantities of farm produce such as an entire field of peppers, cabbage, garlic, or radishes. This was around the end of October just before the winter season of making kimchi. He would wait for a while and then try to resell the produce to a store at the right time to make a profit. I recall he sometimes made money but since this was also a form of gambling, he lost more than he won. He often became greedy, waiting too long and taking chances before he would resell. My dad loved gambling with almost everything he did. When he returned home, he was usually irritated and demanded money from the rest of the family. At this time, our family was not wealthy, but we were better situated than most others. Eventually my father lost his entire share of the family inheritance through gambling.

Grandpa was the polar opposite of my aggressive father. Grandpa felt powerless and would just become passive because he couldn't control Dad's behaviors. He was well aware that our family was in danger of losing everything, but Grandpa would simply walk away when my dad became abusive.

Dad's siblings were also nothing like him. They didn't drink or gamble. They were caring and responsible for their families. They also respected their parents and their elder brother. My two uncles were much younger than my dad, (my oldest uncle was ten years younger, and my other uncle was 16 years younger). At the time, girls did not have many rights in family matters. Men were always first, as it was a man's world. However, Grandma was in charge of dealing with our household issues. She was the only family member who dared oppose my father. She tried her best, but it was hard dealing with her stubborn son. Dad was cruel and looked down on her, probably because she was a woman. He was always arguing with her and demanded that things go his way. Even at my young age, I recognized that the entire family was afraid of my dad, who was violent and unpredictable.

I remember living in constant terror of him. One of my earliest memories was when I was about two and a half years old. I was at home playing outside with my grandmother. Mom was working in the garden while carrying my younger brother Seok-Gu on her back. Dad returned from a lengthy absence and immediately began arguing with Grandma. I didn't understand then, but my father was demanding more money because he had lost it all gambling again. I recall hiding and hearing Dad yelling at Grandma, which made me even more terrified. I ran to my grandmother for comfort. As I approached her, Dad stuck his foot out and tripped me. Then he yelled something along the lines of, "Stay away, and don't ever walk in front of me!" I frantically screamed and stood up shaking, unable to move from fear. I didn't want to be near him since he was so frightening. Grandma yelled at him and rushed to pick me up. In stressful moments like this she was often my savior. Grandma and I talked about that incident later as I grew older.

My brother Seok-Gu was born a little after I was two years old. Despite Seok-Gu's good health, taking care of both of us was too much for my mom with all the household chores. Grandma began to look after me and I slept with her at night and spent most of the daytime in her company. I understood from a young age that my mom was ill-equipped to defend herself from Dad. My father was continually mean to her and treated her poorly, but she never seemed to say anything back to him.

Mom was overwhelmed by her physical responsibilities and rarely smiled. She appeared to be angry most of the time. As I got older, Mom slipped into a cycle of powerlessness and anxiety, putting little Seok-Gu in a terrible position. My

36

grandparents' love for me at least provided a solid foundation. Eventually, Grandma started to take care of Seok-Gu, too, because Mom became pregnant again. By then, Mom had lost many babies, some stillborn, others dying very young. I started asking why she was continually having more babies. We didn't have the money to feed them, so I questioned why she would keep getting pregnant. I also talked with Grandma about how my mom appeared so ignorant, but she would just say you will understand when you are older. I was too naive then and did not know much at that age - I think I was about eight years old at the time. As I grew a little older, all I knew was that every time Dad returned home and stayed for a little while, Mom would become pregnant. Sadly, he was never at home by the time the babies were born.

It seemed to me that Mom was on the verge of having a nervous breakdown. Unfortunately, she would often take it out on me. She would yell at me and rarely show me tenderness. I reasoned that if I was a good girl, maybe things would change, so when I was about seven or eight, I started helping Mom with her chores. As I grew older, Mom would wake me up first thing in the morning and send me to fetch water to warm on the stove while she, Seok-Gu, and the others were still in bed. I did the dishes and all the other household chores. Mom was too depressed to get up many mornings. I expected this to cheer her up, but she remained pessimistic. I was unable to play or do things that my neighbor friends did because I was expected to help my mother, who became increasingly reliant on me as I grew older. She seemed to have completely forgotten that I was still a child.

As Seok-Gu and I grew older, we noticed that Dad would stay at home for a few days if he didn't have any money. We despised him for this since he drank every day and made everyone miserable. We often wondered why Dad was mean to us but so nice to people outside the family. Sadly, they didn't even see that it was all fake. Hiding your true feelings is embedded in the old Korean Yi dynasty culture that was learned over many generations. Even though he was such a hypocrite, none of us dared say a word because we were afraid of him. Dad's tantrums become more frequent over time. They were usually aimed at Mom, who was unable to stand up to him.

Sue (10 years old), Mom, Hong-Gu & Seok-Gu

Dad began to target Seok-Gu as my brother grew older. If he had a favorite, it was me (I think because I'm the only one who stayed up to help him until he fell asleep). I certainly did not regard it as a privilege. I hated it whenever Dad created problems, but I would be the one to confront him in an effort to save Mom from being beaten. I would often drag him home after he had been in a fight, abandoned on the streets, or in a gutter due to gambling debts. I would ask Seok-Gu, even beg him, to go with me to get Dad. He'd usually run away and hide so well that I couldn't find him anywhere.

Eventually I stopped asking Seok-Gu to help me go get Dad and just did it myself. Whenever Dad came home late at night drunk and angry, it seemed everyone including our neighbors could hear him. His yelling was so loud that his voice projected a long way late in the night. For our family, there was usually no other choice but to hide in the shed until he fell into a deep sleep. I was the only one who would try to stay awake and then try to calm him down to save my mother from Dad's rage. As soon as he saw Mom, he would usually start beating her badly. This happened so often when he was home, it seemed like almost every other day. I often thought about running away from my miserable life. I heard that some girls in my village would work in a factory in the city to make a little money. At times I thought about doing that, but when I looked at my mother and all my little brothers' faces, I just couldn't leave. I felt I had to help my mom around the house and take care of my brothers.

To make money, Mom went to the market to buy vegetables and fruit, then divided them into little bags. Afterwards she would sit in a corner of the marketplace to try to make a living by reselling the vegetables and fruit. That was the only way we could survive in those days. When Dad came home drunk, he would tell me what he wanted to eat or drink, and I did my best to serve him. I would occasionally massage or scratch his back as he requested. This went on from when I was quite young, around age 6 to 15. I'm sure that this long period of hopelessness in my childhood helped form my strong, stubborn character and perseverance.

On my Dad's side brothers, cousins and aunts

More cousins and aunts

Chapter 6
Conversion to Christianity

Christianity arrived in Korea between 135 and 150 years ago. Most missionaries were from America. Because Buddhism and Confucianism were the main Korean religions, many of the early missionaries faced a lot of persecution. Some of them became martyrs, including the Koreans who became first-generation Christians.

There were only about three Christian families in my area who were Catholic, Methodist, or a branch of the Methodist denomination known as the Evangelical Holiness Church. The majority of Koreans practiced Confucianism mixed with Buddhism. Buddhists believed that human existence is one of suffering and that the only way to obtain enlightenment or nirvana was by meditation as well as spiritual and physical effort. Its adherents worship multiple gods; in other words, they are polytheistic. They believed in demons and ancestral spirits. Many Koreans also practiced Confucianism, with ancestor worship, which emphasized personal morality, but they actually placed more value on outward appearance and rituals.

Buddhism, Confucianism, and Shamanism practices were frequently combined all together.

Family ancestral rituals included ceremonies held once a year on the anniversary of the death of the person being honored (Jesa), and both my mother's and father's family held tea rites on major holidays. Charye is a memorial service for one's ancestors that is performed during Seollal (Lunar New Year's Day), Chuseok (Korean Thanksgiving Day) and other traditional Korean holidays. It is a form of ancestral worship and an expression of gratitude to one's ancestors. Charye was performed for the last four generations of one's ancestors. The family's eldest son was supposed to host the service according to clan rules. Seasonal rites and ceremonial practices are fairly prevalent in modern Korea even now. The family habitually obeyed celestial norms as well as their traditions, and they were very superstitious. For instance, I recall family members putting salt in front of their homes to ward off evil spirits as well as holding séances and making food sacrifices to their ancestors. Another important consideration was the date of family events, travel, or moves and we always consulted with shamans or fortune tellers for advice. This was before our family converted to Christianity.

My father, on the other hand, seemed totally unconcerned about any religion. He appeared interested only in drinking, gambling, and making a fortune quickly. My mother's parents were firm believers in a blend of Confucianism and Buddhism. Their convictions kept Mom from abandoning my father. When Mom expressed her dissatisfaction to her parents, they let her know she couldn't return home because she was a married woman now. They told her that her home was with her husband, regardless of how he behaved, and that she would have to be loyal to Dad until death. If Mom would leave Dad or divorce him, she couldn't take her children with her because in Korean society they usually belonged to the man. (This view in Korean culture has slowly changed). Mom was well aware of this custom and was told she'd lose all her children and never see them again. I knew Mom would never leave us, and there was also no way she could take care of us kids on her own. But I never heard her complain about her parents.

Meanwhile, my father's youngest sister Jong-Lim developed an illness that caused the skin over much of her body to be covered in white itchy patches and scabs. She became angry and depressed, and never wanted to leave home. Grandma tried everything to help her get better with traditional herbal medicine. She believed in ritual prayers for healing, but nothing worked. When Jong-Lim was about 13 years old, a preacher and a group from the Evangelical Holiness Church came to our village to share their faith. They had walked an hour from the city and told Grandma about their crusade, inviting her to bring Jong-Lim so they could pray for her together. Grandma took Jong-Lim to the church meetings, where they spent a week learning more about Christianity. They were excited about the Bible's message of Jesus healing the sick. It was the first time Grandma and Jong-Lim heard the message of Jesus. They followed the revival to a nearby city to attend more meetings. They both experienced the Holy Spirit throughout the crusade. The pastor's name at the crusade was Sung Bong Yi. He was a well-known Korean charismatic Christian revival pastor and Bible instructor of that era, similar to D.L. Moody in the U.S. Jong-Lim's bitter, angry spirit was cleansed over the course of a week and her skin condition improved steadily over time.

After this experience, Grandma and Jong-Lim were very happy and changed into completely different people, and my two uncles also started attending church with them. Grandma and Jong-Lim began to witness to all our neighbor friends, and many in the village became Christians. My grandma's conversion to Christianity was a watershed moment in our family's history for which I am so grateful. I was only about 4-5 years old, but I made up my mind then that I would be a Christian, even though I didn't know much about it. I just knew I wanted to be a Christian when I grew up and was hungry to know more about God ever since then. Mom, along with the majority of our family, eventually became Christians over the years. Surprisingly, Dad never grumbled about us going to church, but he didn't want anything to do with any religion. He only believed in luck and kept hoping to become rich by gambling. At first Mom didn't go to church because she was afraid Dad might be angry at her. She was also intimidated by the congregant's more modern lifestyles, so she felt like she didn't belong. Later Mom started attending the Catholic church close by. Mom told me that they were very nice to her and she felt very peaceful when she attended. I was very happy for her at the time. When she came to America, she enjoyed going to church with me.

After my grandmother turned to Christianity, she became friends with another church family who had fled from North Korea - their family name was Jang. They were well-educated, fun and knowledgeable, and one of the sons played the violin beautifully. It was the first time I had ever heard the sound of a violin. My father's younger brother, Uncle Jong-Su, was very good-looking and had a wonderful singing voice. He was also extroverted and charismatic, popular wherever he went. He became our church's choir leader before he left our family home. My two uncles became close to the Jang family's two sons, who were the same age. They also had a daughter who was my Aunt Jong-Lim's age, and they went to school together. They all became very close friends. Grandma told me that the Jang family was running away from communist North Korea, and lived quietly in my village because they were Christians. Everyone in my village knew that they were from North Korea, but they did not want to fight on either side. Communists were hiding all over Korea during this period, but most people didn't know who was a Communist. Later during the conflict of the war, all four men, my two uncles and the two Jang brothers from North Korea, left our hometown one by one. They fled somewhere near Seoul with a missionary from America to hide and study, but I didn't know exactly where they went or what they were doing. Children were not supposed to ask a lot of questions, so we really didn't know much about what was going on with the grown-ups.

I learned later that the Jang sons were training to become pastors. Uncle Jong-Su also studied as they did but later, he decided to study other subjects. I am not sure exactly what my uncle did, but he was gone for a long time, about 12 to 15 years. He was probably studying at a mission Bible college and working with the missionaries. All I knew was Uncle Jong-Su spoke very good English and collaborated with a missionary from the U.S. to establish an orphanage in Paju near an U.S. Army base after the war. I heard there were many orphans everywhere. He helped people in a variety of ways including translating for civilians as well as finding or providing work for others. My uncle then discovered he could contract and open a business on the U.S. military base. He purchased a barbershop, started making money, growing it to six employees. This allowed him to work on other ventures around the U.S. military base. By the time I got there, he was married with a son. He was still the choir director in his Presbyterian church. He was a very busy man.

According to a November, 2022, research, South Korea is over 30% Christian (20% Protestant, 11% Catholic) and only 17% Buddhist. In the U.S., Korean American immigrants are overwhelmingly Christian - between 60% and 65%.

Chapter 7
Leaving the Family Home

When I was around seven years old, Uncle Jong-Seok returned from Seoul, where he'd been staying with Uncle Jong-Su. He intended to marry one of the local girls from another church near our village. Uncle Jong-Seok was not sure how much land he was entitled to because Dad had already sold off portions of my grandparents' land. Meanwhile my father got into another fight with his parents over how to divide the inheritance and shamelessly demanded even more for himself. Uncle Jong-Seok finally told my father that he would give up half of his share on one condition: that my father would leave, take his family and never come back. In return, my uncle would stay in the family house and take care of their parents and all the household responsibilities. The youngest Uncle Jong-Su did not want any of his share, and he gave it to his brother Jong-Seok.

Uncle Jong-Seok was very different from my dad. He was a hardworking, handy family man. He never drank alcohol or smoked in his life. He was a loving good father, an elder for his Presbyterian church, honest in all his dealings and wise with his money. He started a big chicken farm and became a beekeeper too, along with many other ongoing projects. Over time the value of the property increased because he took good care of it and made many improvements.

Dad was happy and relieved to leave the family home with a considerable amount of the money. He rented a run-down room in a nearby village and took Mom, Seok-Gu, and me to live there. He gave Mom a little money, then told her he would be back as soon as he found a place to live in Seoul. He looked very excited when he left, taking the rest of the money. He always said that he wanted to go live in Seoul since he hated living in the country. After he took off we did not see him again for many months. This is when we started to experience real poverty and the beginning of our downward spiral. Even though we were hungry most of the time in our new living arrangements, Seok-Gu and I were happier whenever Dad was gone for long periods of time.

Even though Mom was depressed, she worked as hard as she could to provide for our family and to survive without Dad. This time Dad was gone for a long time. There were just three of us in those days: Mom, Seok-Gu and me. Mom would leave the house first thing in the morning in search of work. She frequently helped farmers by tending to their gardens in exchange for vegetables, apples or other fruits. I recall her working for a farmer who was a distant relative with an apple orchard. Meanwhile mom was pregnant. Her stomach grew big and she went through a lot of trouble giving birth to a daughter, but for some reason she died less than a week later. Of course Dad wasn't home, as usual. We were all very sad for a while, but Mom had to figure out how to survive the winter with two kids. She would ride the train to the neighboring city to buy large boxes of seaweed to resell at the market. Whenever Mom had extra time, she would take Seok-Gu and me up the mountains to collect sticks, pinecones, pine needles and dried grass so we could cook and heat our rooms. We rarely saw her smile or happy.

I always felt sorry for Mom because she had no friends and always had to work in the market or the fields. I saw she was apprehensive about everything, and her hands would shake when she attempted to get through the day. Mom was also devastated by the death of her children, but she had no family or friends close by to help and support her - her family lived far away. Going to the market was not only a way for her to make money, but it also gave her a way to socialize. She was able to meet new people which helped her slowly regain her confidence.

When I turned seven years old it was time for me to go to school, but Dad was gone and had not prepared for my education. So Uncle Jong-Seok enrolled me in school and paid the tuition for a few months. The South Korea government was still so impoverished that families had to pay tuition and buy books, pencils and notebooks for school. Nothing was free and government assistance was not available to anyone. Most children could not even afford to bring lunch to school and as a result many of the children were hungry all the time. It took me an hour to walk to the school, which was built during Japan's occupation. There were three or four separate one-story rectangular buildings located around a courtyard with a large playground. I had a real desire to read and write. I enjoyed history, but I never liked math. Some teachers would punish naughty children by making us stand in the corner or put our hands over our heads in front of the other students for 30-40 minutes. The teachers would hit our palms with a tiny stick. Many of the students were terrified of their teachers. If the parents were poor like mine and could not pay the tuition on time or could not bribe the teacher, there could be more severe punishment. My attendance became sporadic because my parents couldn't pay my tuition on time. My teachers ignored me, and they only seemed to like the children whose parents had money and bribed them often. I am sure that there were some good teachers too, but I didn't have any.

When Seok-Gu was old enough to go to school, his experience was similar to mine. I remember the kids in my class were only children under 10 years old. How did they recognize who had money or who was from a better family? How did they decide to only be friends with the kids whose family had money? Where did they learn to bully those who had nothing and brown nose the teachers? I was not sophisticated and didn't even know how to think like this. When I look back, I was so insecure and timid, afraid to open my mouth to say anything and always answered obediently. As I grew into an adult, I slowly changed to be very strong mentally. When I see things that I think are not right, I am not afraid and am quick to share my opinion. Now I can be a vicious old woman

I remember walking to school with three girls from a neighboring family whose mother had passed away while they were young. Moonja was two years older than me, Sunhee was my age and Moonhea was two years younger. They had two older brothers and one of them went to college in Seoul. Their single father was a responsible family man who did not drink or gamble and played games with his children. When they played with their father they laughed together like good friends. I recall

51

wishing that my father was more like him. I envied their family because they were content with their lives.

I'm still friends with all three sisters who have always remained in my memory, especially the oldest one - Moonja. Moonja and I walked to church service every Sunday as well as Wednesday and Friday nights for many years. Sunhe wasn't much interested in going to church because she was in high school and had her own friends. It took us an hour to walk each way, but it was my only happy time during my otherwise hopeless teenage years. The way back was always dark except when the stars and moon were bright. Sometimes we were afraid to walk in the dark so we sang hymns very loud and prayed all the way home. Later Moonja and Moonhea both became youth pastors at the church. They are all old like me now. Last year in April when I was visiting Korea, I visited them too and we were so happy to see each other, hugging and crying.

I remember winters being really cold. We didn't have any boots, but wore traditional rubber shoes instead. Mom would stuff cotton into our garments to keep us warm. The wood-burning stove in the middle of the classroom never warmed us completely, which made it difficult to concentrate. While in class, I used to worry that my father would come home screaming and belligerent. Because of my fear, I also had trouble sleeping at night, so I would pray to God about my family situation. I wanted Dad to stop drinking and gambling so that we could have a regular life like other families. I graduated from elementary school but did not have the opportunity to continue because of course Dad didn't care to send me. I told myself that I would someday finish my education on my own, but for now I'd have to help my mom.

I also went with Grandma and Aunt Jong-Lim to church once in a while. I enjoyed going to church to sing hymns and listen to the sermon even though I didn't quite understand everything. It gave me a break from my mundane daily existence at home and I felt safe in church. The atmosphere was different there, and people seemed more gentle and happy. I kept telling myself that I would become a Christian, and I would follow the Christian faith. Grandma, Aunt Jong Rim and I prayed for many years for my Dad to quit drinking and gambling and to become a Christian like his brother, so we could live a peaceful normal home life. But for some reason God never answered that prayer and I was disappointed that my faith was shaky for many years.

I thought God is doing whatever he wants to do - it doesn't matter for God, no matter how much we pray to Him. Later when I was working on the U.S. military base, I had to work most Sundays and was so busy that I could not go to church. Nonetheless, whenever I passed by church, I felt that I had to go soon, and started to pray. Oh God help me! I was hungry to know more about God, and I promised myself that I would study the Bible as soon as I had the chance. My first priority would be to get educated and then study the Bible. Grandma told me that our family had followed false gods and shamanism for a long time because they did not know any better. Her belief system had begun to shift as she studied the Bible, so I believed studying the Bible was very important. When Grandma decided to burn their idols and other symbolic items they used to revere, I was very excited and happy because I never liked those things anyway. Our school went on field trips in the spring, and they often took us to Buddhist Temples located in beautiful mountain valleys. Some of the most well-known temples were constructed before the Yi dynasty era. Even though the scenery was beautiful and the people in the temples were cordial, I disliked statues of Buddha and wanted to leave as soon as possible. I knew even at my young age, I would never be a worshiper of Buddha. I'm not criticizing Buddhism; I'm just sharing my experience and that my choice was made at a young age.

My father later returned for a short period. Then my second brother, Heung-gu, was born a year after the baby girl died. My grandparents and Aunt Jong-Lim lived with Jong-Seok in the Yi family home, but Grandma was worried about us and often she walked to our place and brought food for us to eat as we only lived about two miles from our family home.

Dad's actions caused our family to suffer even more, and he often demanded that we go ask Mom's family for extra money. If we didn't go, he would become irate. Mom would take all the kids with her, but as time passed and she had more children, this became impossible. So she started sending me alone to her sister's house, when I was about 13 or 14 years old. I hated going and felt very ashamed. They would welcome me in and seemed to know why I was there, but they never asked any questions. My younger cousins were happy to have me stay with them, but I lacked confidence because I was not in school like they were. I was still thankful and wanted to help them with any housework or chores. I usually stayed for a week to ten days, and they would want me to stay longer. They never let me leave empty-handed, but would send me with money and other small items that I could carry home to Mom. During the long summer vacation, all my other cousins would come from the city to visit our aunt on the farm. There was plenty to do there, and I recall many different fruit trees and gardens with various kinds of melon for us to eat. I was the eldest among my cousins and I

54

always worked, helping my aunt in many ways, so they always welcomed me.

Dad continued his pattern of abandoning us for extended periods of time. I remember a man telling us, "Your dad lives in the next village with another woman." We were unaware of this chatter in our village, and Mom told me to go tell Dad that we needed his help and to bring him home - I was about ten years old. I heard about this village but had never been there. This place, Young Mal, was about four to five miles from our home and had a bad reputation for gambling and drinking. In order to get there, I had to walk a zigzag trail for about three miles through some small hills. As I was walking past a public graveyard, I suddenly remembered a ghost story and started running terrified. I remember that I ended up cracking my rubber shoes. When I finally arrived, I was thirsty and hungry. I had no idea where Dad was so I stopped at a couple different houses to ask strangers if they knew Chong-man Yi. "Go to that house," remarked one man, pointing down the street. I was so exhausted that I collapsed on the doorstep of the house, where I eventually found my dad with another woman. They sat at a small, short-legged Korean-style table. I can still see it in my mind's eye - my recollection of that moment is as vivid as a photograph.

Dad was taken back when he saw me and said, "What are you doing here?!" I wanted to tell him I was there to take him home, but I burst into tears and couldn't say anything. I felt so ashamed. Dad was quiet and simply stated, "Go home now!" He gave me a little bit of money. I finally said to him, "Mom says you need to come home soon. We have a new baby and we don't have any food." Before I left to go home by myself, the woman seemed to feel sorry for me and offered me some food and drink.

At this time in Korean culture, it was not unusual for men to have children with their mistresses so I found it odd that my father never had more children with other women, none that we knew of anyway. I couldn't understand how he could waste his time and money on other women instead of supporting his own family. I recall thinking that Mom should have gone to get Dad, but she lacked courage. She was distraught and felt helpless.

About a year later, we relocated to another rental property in the city of Sangyo-Eap, where we stayed for approximately two years. Whenever Dad got a little extra money, he would say that we were going to move to Seoul, but we never made it there because of his uncontrollable gambling addiction. He didn't want to stop gambling until the last penny was gone. Our family was short on food and often hungry even though Grandma would bring us food whenever she could. This wasn't unusual at the time as there was no government aid. (Big cities of Seoul, Busan, Daejeon and Dagu did receive food and clothing from the United States but country people like us never benefited.) Without Grandma, I know that we would not have made it.

My brother Jeong-Gu was born when I was 13 years old. His birth was complicated because the placenta did not emerge immediately, and a neighbor came to assist. A couple of days went by and Mom's face turned yellow. She kept saying she was going to die, and she told me I had to take care of my siblings. She told me to go get Grandma who lived an hour away. Grandma found the city's only physician who was also a member of her church. Fortunately, he was able to extract the placenta and save Mom. We were all so relieved! We didn't have any money to pay him, but Uncle Jong-Seok was a beekeeper, so

Grandma gave him a big jar of honey which was very valuable back then.

Mom was still frail, and Jeong-Gu needed her care. We were cold and hungry but there was no wood to burn. Grandma knew we were in an impossible situation, so she told us to pack up and come with her. Her voice sounded very determined, and we carried the few belongings all five of us had and walked an hour back to the family home. We moved into Grandma's room without the approval of my uncle and aunt who were caught off guard with our arrival. They were upset because Grandma never asked for permission, but she felt she had no choice. My uncle Jong-Seok was angry with my dad and Grandma because now he had five additional mouths to feed in an overcrowded house. Because of the situation Dad had put us in, Mom and I tried to do as much work around the house as possible. I felt unwanted and ashamed of my father. Our family had created a heavy burden for my uncles and aunts. It seemed that our presence was despised wherever we went.

Chapter 8

Back to the Family Home

It was an extremely stressful time when we came back to the family home. We were humiliated, but we did not have much choice. When Dad finally reappeared, he seemed a little timid and embarrassed at first. But then he began to exclaim that this was his house originally, so he could live in it as long as he wanted. There was a lot of squabbling. Everyone could see that Dad was acting outrageously. Grandpa was so different from my aggressive dad. I think my grandpa was much too passive about everything. He did not want to face my dad or his other sons. After a few months of this living situation, Uncle Jong-Seok finally told my father to stay at the family home and look after my grandparents. He felt he had no choice but to sell his land and leave with all of his belongings. Our family problems were my father's fault again and again. Even though I was young, I still knew that Dad was wrong. Our family ended up living in this same house until 1975 when they came to America.

I was continually asked to go work for Mom's family members or ask them for money. Mom also continued to have children, which meant she had even more work to do. For my brothers and me, the scariest days were when Dad would hit Mom and throw objects at her. We would sit in the corner, heads down, unable to move. We didn't even dare to get up to use the restroom. Seok-Gu would run outside to hide when Dad came home drunk late at night. It was up to me to calm down Dad. I would tell Mom to leave and hide somewhere. We had no police to report Dad's abuse, and there was no place to call to get help. The government would not intervene unless someone was dead.

When I was 14 or 15, Mom began sending me to her brother Young-Hyun's house because they always needed extra help. I did not want to go there, but I had to help my family. My uncle's wife was reluctant to help us because she had her own relatives who needed help too. This time she sent me to work at another friend's house whom she knew a few miles from their place. My uncle had no idea she did this. He assumed she had given me some money and sent me home. I did not blame them for anything. They were very busy people who were preoccupied with their own business and eight children.

After several weeks Mom came to her brother's house to take me home. She had no way of letting my aunt and uncle know that she would be there, so they were surprised to see her. When Mom discovered I wasn't there she became upset with my uncle and aunt. When she arrived at the store where I was working, she informed me that we were leaving. The shopkeeper told me, "If you want to leave, give back the new sweater we just bought for you." Mom yanked the sweater from me and threw it at them and said, "Here's your lousy sweater! I can buy a better one for her." On the way home, she stopped at the store and bought me a new pink cardigan. It was the first time I saw her act like that. That's when I understood my mom genuinely cared about me.

Grandma lived with us for a few months in the family home until she couldn't stand arguing with Dad anymore. She frequently visited my younger uncle Jong-Su. He was a part-time interpreter for civilian workers for the United States military. Grandma asked Jong-Su if he could help locate a job for me on the U.S. military base because he had helped others find work. Dad was home more frequently and for longer amounts of time for some unknown reason. This made our lives even more miserable, and we were further devastated when Grandma left us to live with Uncle Jong-Su.

My grandfather would likewise disappear for extended periods of time, but no one knew where he went. We imagined he was in the next town to see his daughter or other relatives since he had done this before. When Grandpa was gone during this time, I worried whether he would return or be gone forever. After the Korean war, I often heard of people simply disappearing. Grandpa did not want to ever confront my father ever. As time went on, I became more aware of the seriousness of the situation. I recall looking down the road and hoping to see him walking back home.

Seok-Gu and I fought frequently because it appeared to me that he was unconcerned about our family problems. He always said "no" when I asked for help. He would be gone for the entire day and return home for dinner. Maybe he was just trying to distance himself so it wouldn't hurt as badly. I tried to give him suggestions on how he could help improve our family and his life. He always said he didn't care about anything. He was only two years my junior but we could not be more different. I began to feel sad for Seok-Gu as time passed because I recognized how difficult his life was. Most other fathers were very close to their sons as boys were very important in Korean culture, but my dad completely ignored him from the beginning and treated him badly. That's why Seok-Gu always ran away and hid whenever Dad came home. On the other hand, I tried to stay positive. I kept thinking someday things would get better. I would often dream of having a nice house with a lot of nice clothes and shoes for my mother. I never thought about clothes for me or my own future. I would tell myself, "With God's help, I will improve our family's situation so we won't be poor." When I'd ask Seok-Gu what he was thinking, he'd answer that he only wanted to get away from Dad. I was frustrated, but I agreed with this sentiment. Those were hopeless and miserable times throughout our teenage years from ages 10 to 17.

An unforgettable event happened when I was around 15 years old. Dad returned home late one night drunk and angry, having lost all his money again. Whenever he was in this state, he would come home screaming that the next time he would win everything. He would shout "monjori" (몽조리) loudly walking down the street and waking all the neighbors. It was Korean slang that he used which actually meant he would take it all. This happened so frequently that all the villagers and even young kids would comment, "Here comes Monjori!" That particular night we all escaped outside through the back door, while Dad was still shouting and sitting out on the deck. Seok-Gu said, "I wish he was dead." We didn't realize it at the time, but Dad must have heard it and assumed that it was me. I walked out on the deck to try calming him as usual, but to my astonishment he grabbed me and knocked me down to the ground. He grabbed a stick with his other hand and began hitting me. Mom ran out and tried to stop him which enraged him even more, and he began to beat and kick her. Mom kept sobbing and called for Seok-Gu to help, but he had vanished. Dad continued to beat me until I could not move. He eventually stopped and walked away. Mom dragged me inside. My ribs were bruised and possibly broken, and I had trouble breathing for over a month.

When I told Seok-Gu I was writing my memoirs, he said I should include this event even though I don't like to think about it. This was the first and only time Dad beat me since I was the only one in the family he trusted. I was the one who took care of him when he came home drunk and angry. I stayed with him, and I didn't run away. He must have been shocked and felt betrayed, thinking I wanted him dead. Dad never talked about that night again. To my knowledge, he never found out it was actually Seok-Gu who cursed him, but I still remained his favorite and the one he turned to. Many years later, Seok-Gu apologized profusely to me, even in recent months. Seok-Gu now lives in Denver, Colorado. He has a lovely daughter and son with two grandkids.

When Heung-Gu first entered school, he was very popular and soon developed a close friendship with one of his wealthy classmates in our village. Seeing this, I was convinced that Heung-Gu was the sharpest and most attractive in his class. He would be the hope for our future. I was so desperate for a good son to save our mother. Oh, how naive I was to think like that, but in our culture the sons were the head of the family, and the daughter would eventually leave to live with and serve her husband's family. My plan was to work hard to support Heung-Gu's education so he could grow up to be a good man. I also hoped my two younger brothers, Jeong-Gu and Tae-Gu, would help take care of Mom. I wanted them all to have a good education and grow up to become responsible men unlike my dad.

Heung-Gu's death from colon cancer in 2019 still breaks my heart. It's especially sad, considering he was ten years younger than me. How I loved him when we were growing up. He never gave me any trouble and was my favorite sibling. Due to Covid limitations, I was unable to visit him in the hospital and could only FaceTime with him over the phone. I still have an aching heart whenever I think about him.

Grandpa left when I was 15 and never returned. The government authorities attempted to assist us find him, but they were preoccupied with other issues and did not search for long. We were unable to locate him on our own, and we finally concluded that he died, but we had no idea how or where. I primarily blamed my father, but also his siblings. I wish they would have shown greater concern for their parents. My grandpa's disappearance was a big stain on our Yi family. Grandma now lived with Uncle Jong-Su in the city of Paju and would visit us occasionally.

Although the war officially ended when the Communists were driven back to North Korea, the country was still divided in two. The majority of individuals continued to struggle. In 1962 President Park started building factories in various cities to create jobs and help the country recover from war and poverty. This encouraged young people to leave the countryside and move to the cities. My dad still talked about leaving our village to start a business. He always had lots of ideas but no plans to do manual labor in the fields or a factory. He could never make his impossible dreams come true since he wasn't willing to start out small or put in the work. Dad often took big risks because he was greedy and wanted success quickly.

Chapter 9
An Invitation

In 1961, when I was 17 years old, Uncle Jong-Su invited me to live with him and his wife in Paju, a small city by a U.S. military installation near North Korea. South Korea was still impoverished and the government and people struggled to survive. People wanted to stay close to U.S. military bases where they could find jobs or small business opportunities. When Uncle Jong-Su became a Christian, he learned English from the missionaries. This ability allowed him to recommend people for employment on the military base, and he was able to find jobs for family and friends. Grandma noticed this as she was now living with him and asked him if he could hire or train me for a job. I found out later that my Grandma had been nagging my uncle for this favor for a long time. Uncle Jong- Su told Grandma I was not ready for that kind of job yet. He told Grandma I needed to learn many skills first. After all, I was just a country girl, but my grandma never gave up on me. She knew me better than anyone. She believed in me, so she didn't care that I wasn't ready or capable. My uncle eventually asked me to come live with them, so he could personally teach and train me. It was a difficult decision because I was concerned about Mom and my brothers, but I finally accepted my uncle's invitation. My decision to leave home was yet another pivotal moment in my life.

Sue and Grandma

Uncle Jong-Su

Paju was far away from my hometown. It took most of the day to get there as it required a four or five-hour train ride, a three-hour ride on multiple buses with another hour on foot. (Today it is just one 2½ hour car ride.) I was planning to go alone, but Dad showed up out of the blue and said he was taking me to my uncle's house. I was very unhappy about this, but I couldn't stop him. I was miserable all day traveling with him. He wanted to control everything, and this just gave him an excuse to go ask his brother for money again.

Sue when she first came to Paju

Paju was so different from my hometown; the pace was faster and busier. Life in Paju seemed more complicated to me. I had to change my mindset and learn quickly to catch up to city life. Grandma encouraged me to be patient and appreciative since this was a great opportunity for my future.

For the first year, I stayed with my uncle and aunt in a house with 4 bedrooms and a courtyard. It was a modern new house, which felt like a luxury. Grandma was getting older, but her mind remained bright while she was living with them. I was relieved to see her again, and it became my responsibility to look after her during my stay, but it was also a real privilege.

68

Uncle Jong-Su arranged for private tutors to help me learn English and typing so that I could work at a U.S. Army base. He told Grandma that I was smart and hard-working so he believed I could catch on quickly. He hoped he could find me a position at one of the United States army facilities that remained after the war. Korean civilians worked in a variety of capacities on these bases. Men polished shoes, did laundry, cleaned rooms, made meals, worked in the PX (post exchange) store, craft shop, library, cafeteria, club or barbershop. The women who could type well were able to work in the army offices. Uncle Jong-Su was well-connected. He appeared to know everyone on the base and was able to obtain employment for several relatives, including his wife's family. He also found jobs for his sister's husband, his brother Jong-Seok, and eventually me. Learning English was more challenging than I anticipated. (Although I consider myself a quick learner for most things, I'm not as skilled as I'd like to be with English. After 52 years of living in America, I still find it much easier to speak and write in Korean which has made writing this memoir in English difficult.)

My uncle made sure I learned how to type and operate a cash register. He said that more knowledge and experience would give me a better chance at getting a job. My studies and training took up a large portion of my day, and then I was expected to help my aunt with the housework in the evening. After almost a year of training in many different areas, my uncle determined that I was ready to get a job, and he put in applications to a few places for me.

After a couple of weeks, my uncle told me to get a complete physical because I had an interview at a small craft shop on the base. A week later, the shop manager let my uncle know that I could start work. I was nervous and worried, but just like Uncle Jong-Su had told me, it was simple. The manager was a kind middle-aged Korean man who trained me on everything the job required. I did not have to talk too much, but just answer a few questions that I might be asked. I also did a little dusting and cleaning if needed, as well as organizing the books and materials in the shop. The soldiers would work on projects like woodworking, drawing and painting or write and read. I would pick up after they left for the day, but they usually cleaned up themselves, so there wasn't much for me to do and the job became boring. The U.S. soldiers who came to the shop were both young and older, and sometimes we had officers like Captains and Lieutenants, but I noticed they all were well mannered and gentlemanly. My hours were from 11 am to 4 pm daily, 5 days a week. In my free time I started to read a little. The salary was much lower than other jobs, but I was still very thankful because I now had an opportunity to advance to other opportunities once I was employed on the base. It all depended on me and how I performed my duties.

One thing I really liked about my first job was that I could check out classic books translated into Korean and take them home to read every night. These books were meant for college-educated Korean soldiers who worked on the U.S. military base. At that time it was difficult to find these classic books written in Korean so this gave me the opportunity to read many great books. The first book I read was *The Good Earth* by Pearl Buck.

The whole world opened up to me through other stories by Pearl Buck such as *East Wind West Wind* and *The Enemy*. Among other famous books, I enjoyed reading the following: *Gone with the Wind*, *Doctor Zhivago*, Leo Tolstoy's *What Men Live By*, Dostoevsky's *Crime and Punishment* as well as *The Idiot*, and Hemingway's *The Old Man and the Sea*. Reading gave me confidence, hope, and joy. I still believe that reading these books was the best education for me thus far in my life. My favorite writers were Pearl Buck and Fyodor Dostoevsky.

Even though I wanted to work in the cafeteria since the compensation was better, my uncle believed I still needed more training, and he told me to keep studying English. After five months in the craft shop, he got me a position at his barber shop, where they offered haircuts and shaving services. He also ran a shoe polish business next to the barbershop. There were six employees besides me. I began by sweeping and scrubbing the floor, cleaning and washing towels, sanitizing the hair cutting tools, and finally working my way up to cashier.

Two women from Jeju Island worked at the shop and lived with my uncle, so I shared a room with them. They taught me a lot because they were 5 or 6 years older than me and had dominant personalities. Their mother was a Haenyeo (female divers in the South Korean province of Jeju Island whose livelihood consisted of harvesting a variety of mollusks, seaweed, and other sea life from the bottom of the ocean.) These two girls were both trained to dive when they were young, so they were physically very strong. Jeju Island's culture states that women go out to work to earn money, while men stay at home and do the housework. It's very different from inland Korean culture. There are still some female divers in Jeju Island today.

Sue as a waitress in Korea

Chapter 10
Independence

After a year of working, I could now afford to live on my own. I rented a one-room apartment and invited Grandma to stay with me. We slept on pads on the floor. That was what everyone had to do; not many people had beds, because the rooms were small.

I gradually made some friends with my coworkers. I met a few other Koreans who worked in the cafeteria and discovered they were making four times as much as I did in the craft shop. Officers' clubs and NCO (non-commissioned officer) clubs required bartenders, cooks, and waiters. It was generally known that these jobs were in higher demand due to better salaries and tips. At the time, my goal was to make more money, so I applied for a job at the club. A couple months later, I was working as a waitress in the club and cafeteria, where I worked from around 1962 through 1965. But the job was not as easy as my first two jobs. It took a few weeks for me to be comfortable. I learned diligently by shadowing another woman who worked there. I had to be fast and stay focused all the time. I learned about food sanitation rules while working there. We didn't have running water in the kitchen or bathrooms in our village when I was growing up, so we didn't want to waste any of the water because we had to carry it from a public well. I had a lot to learn about cleanliness practices which are automatic habits for me today such as frequently washing hands.

Bill when we first met

Standard meals were served in the mess hall on the base but soldiers frequently complained that the food there wasn't very tasty even though it was free. Soldiers could, however, purchase special meals such as fried chicken, steak, tuna fish, club sandwiches, or hamburgers from the cafeteria. Many seemed to enjoy ham or grilled cheese sandwiches, although these foods were all unfamiliar to me.

The club had many uses as a multi-purpose facility for eating, drinking, playing cards and games, and even meetings. Once or twice a month Korean celebrities would come from Seoul to sing, dance and put on magic, music or comedy shows for the American soldiers stationed here. Soldiers also brought Korean girls from nearby villages to the base. I was shocked to see that there were areas in the villages exclusively for women and I soon discovered that these women were prostitutes. I didn't judge them because they were just trying to survive and may not have had other options to earn a living, and they looked happy. It was, however, perplexing to me why the American and Korean governments permitted this to go on. The women even carried ID cards showing who they were and were checked regularly by doctors, so their activities could be sanctioned legally. I gradually realized that wherever there were a lot of men, there would be a lot of women too. I learned about life fast.

When Seok-Gu was a teenager and needed money, he would sometimes stay with me. It was still difficult to obtain work in the villages, and he was unable to find a job. He had a beautiful singing voice and aspired to be a professional singer. I gave him tuition to attend a singing school for a year so he could do something meaningful and boost his self-esteem. The next time he came to see me, I asked him how school was going, but he admitted he'd been scammed by a con-man and the money was now gone. This was common in Korea at the time. A few days after Seok-Gu left, I discovered that my small radio that I'd just purchased was missing. I had been so proud to show it to him, but he must have been so desperate to take it. I could hardly believe he'd stolen it, and I was furious. I didn't see Seok-Gu much after that. Mom told me later that he'd dropped out of the singing school and was now working around our family house. Because there was so much competition, people had to be ambitious. Without a father to direct and guide him, Seok-Gu never developed many goals or had anything to look forward to. He told me once he thought he'd be better off as a war orphan because then at least he could get support from the orphanage. I reminded him that he still had many chances to make his mark.

When he was old enough to join the army, Seok-Gu volunteered to fight in the Vietnam War. We heard that if Koreans fought in the Vietnam War, the American administration would pay the Korean government since more soldiers were needed.

Over 320,000 South Korean males volunteered to serve alongside American soldiers in Vietnam from 1964 to 1973. Both governments made a deal because the Korean government needed money for our country. Over 5,000 of these Korean men were killed. The average monthly compensation for military duty in Vietnam was $37.50, but the South Korean government took most of it. The following is an excerpt from a September 13, 1970 *New York Times* story.

> *"A Senate Foreign Relations subcommittee discloses today that the dispatch of 50,000 South Korean soldiers to fight in South Vietnam had cost the U.S. more than $1 billion in the last five years. The agreement under which that sum*

was spent covered direct support for the troops, such as overseas allowances, arms, equipment and rations. It further covered a wide range of other assistance, including modernization of South Korean forces in their own country, procurement of military goods in South Korea for U.S. forces in South Vietnam, expanded work for South Korean contractors in South Vietnam, and financial aid."

Thankfully, Seok-Gu survived and returned home safely. We were very happy. However, Seok-Gu paid a high personal cost for his duty as he lost his singing voice due to an infection contracted while working in the communication section. Recently, Seok-Gu told me that the South Korean government started paying him $250 every month for the rest of his life for his one-year service in the Vietnam War. I realized that the Korean government must be substantially wealthier now.

All the years I was working, I sent money home trying to ensure that some of it was used to pay for my three brothers' education. In 1965, Heung-Gu came to live with me during his summer break after finishing middle school. He would be starting high school that autumn and I assumed there would be greater options in the city. Unfortunately, I was transferred to another base in a nearby city so I was unable to enroll Heung-Gu in a city high school. I was often moved to different bases to work. Heung-Gu had to go back home and attend school there. My parents' home life remained difficult, so he would leave most of the time and stay with a friend closer to school whenever he could.

Chong-Hee (Sue Sackrider)

In 1968, when I was 22 years old, my next position was on a base near the DMZ, but it was on the front lines, close to North Korea. Because the compensation was much higher, I chose to work there for two years. I thought since the South and North weren't actively fighting I wasn't in any danger. There were special dark green U.S. military buses that would take 12 women from a designated place to our respective club. This bus was only for U.S. military soldiers and U.S. military employees. We had to cross the Imjin river, which was about a half-mile long. The Imjin River flowed north to south, traversing the DMZ and connecting with Seoul's Han River. Everyone's ID was checked at both ends of the bridge - before the bus crossed and when we got across, imposing guards at the security gates checked our ID again. We were then taken to our separate clubs - two of us for each club.

Un, my dearest friend, rode the bus with me but worked at another base. The bases were located not too far from each other, about a half mile or a little less. We could see soldiers with guns guarding outside, but we were not afraid. Each club had about eight to ten slot machines and the soldiers came to gamble whenever they had free time. Three or four Korean men were employed in each club as the manager, cook, bartender, and janitor, and they would stay overnight sometimes if they wanted to. My job started at 11 am and ended around 7 pm. I would help in the kitchen and bar area, dusting and cleaning tables and chairs when it wasn't busy. I suppose it was similar to any restaurant and bar waitressing job in the U.S. The civilian employees were not allowed to go outside of the building, so there wasn't anyone walking around outside. It still felt like normal, peaceful everyday life. Un and I were the youngest of the women, and we learned a lot from the older ladies who had more experience. They were a big help to us if we needed to know anything. After two years of working at the DMZ, many Korean civilians started getting laid off because the U.S. soldiers were being removed from the frontlines. The ROC Korean army was replaced with the U.S. army. I was fortunate to be one of the few who was chosen to join the other U.S. troops in the rear, and to continue working for this U.S. army base.

While I was working at the DMZ, I signed a two-year contract, so I knew I would live at the same place for at least two years. I brought Jeong-Gu and Tae-Gu to live with me then because I still thought they would have a better chance with schooling in the city and I wanted them to experience city life. They had never traveled far from our hometown or seen much more than a lot of rice patties. I enrolled them in a middle school and they didn't have any problems changing schools. However, I soon discovered they were spending all their time reading comics at the comic book store with new friends they met in school, instead of doing their homework. At that time reading comic books was very popular with kids. Comic book stores were everywhere in the city, but not in my home village, so my brothers got really excited and quickly became addicted. I usually didn't get home until 9:30pm, but they were still out at the comic book store. I found out that they would go there straight after school, and they were constantly drawing different comic characters. I wanted them to study hard in school so they would be able to go to college. I was desperate to help my brothers obtain a good education but discovering this made me feel helpless once again. I advised them that they needed to study every day if they wanted to improve their life. I was upset with Jeong-Gu that he introduced comic books to our younger brother Tae-Gu. I tried talking to them, punishing them, and even threatening them but nothing worked. They continued to spend all of their time after school at the comic book store. I couldn't control them and I was frustrated but didn't know what to do. I thought that I would have to send them back home.

A few days later, I walked past a Tae Kwon Do school on my way to work. I thought this would be better than their comic book addiction, so I suggested it to them the next day, and they reluctantly agreed to try it out. I signed them both up and the instructor showed them what the other students were working on, then told them to come every day after school to practice on their own before class started. They quickly caught up to the other students and surpassed them, then started competing with another city as a team. Tae Kwon Do helped them conquer their comic book habit, and they seemed much more confident in themselves. I was very thankful that I didn't have to worry about the comic book problem anymore.

About a year later, I was transferred to work at another army base, where I met my future husband Bill. This place was pretty close to where we lived, so I was happy that we didn't have to move again. But in just seven months, I had to quit my job and was preparing to get married. Jeong-Gu and Tae-Gu returned back home to the country school they used to attend and continued to practice Tae Kwon Do on their own. They both excelled in middle school as well as high school sports, including soccer. They were also talented artists, continuing to draw as a hobby. They did well in school which made me happy.

Soon my friend Un, began dating an American soldier. She told me that if we didn't start thinking seriously about our future, we'd be out of work when the American soldiers left. I recognized that all American soldiers would most certainly return to the United States, and that I might not always have this job. I became more concerned about my family and future. I started to pray to God for help and guidance. I had been regularly saving for a few years, so I had a decent amount of money in the bank. I thought I could open some kind of small retail business in the city if I lost my job. A couple of months later, Un quit her job and got married to the American soldier. Soon after, her husband was transferred to another country - he was a career soldier. She went to America by herself to stay with her in-laws in Los Angeles, California while she waited for her husband to come home. Un's experience had a big impact on my life.

Chapter 11
A Turning Point

At the time, I was unaware how significant this latest transfer to another army base would prove to be in my life. Compared to other locations, the atmosphere here felt more relaxed, but my salary was significantly lower. While many soldiers left the base to go out and party in the nearby towns whenever they had free time, others spent their leave time in the cafeteria talking and playing cards. I was their server but I wasn't very attentive because I was the only waitress and very busy, as well as helped out in the kitchen. However, as time went on, I noticed one particular group of five guys who frequently played cards in the cafeteria that seemed well-mannered. I later learned that this group was engaged in the same project to assemble atomic bombs. This project required them to leave the base for special training. The group continued to frequent the cafeteria and enjoyed making jokes, so we sometimes made small talk. Soldiers would often ask me about my life and would share stories and photos of their loved ones whom they were missing back home.

I was not supposed to chat much with customers, but we slowly developed a closer relationship. At the time, I was working almost every day with one Sunday off a month. It was important for me to work as much as possible so that I could help my family, and I was also saving money monthly in the bank. When they inquired how long I had been employed at the base, I learned that one of the men, Bill Sackrider, had been transferred to the base on the same day I started working there. Bill was tall, handsome, and appeared to be very stable. He showed me photos of his parents, brother, and grandparents - he told me that he did not have a girlfriend. He was straight forward with a good sense of humor.

I gradually learned more about Bill's life in the U.S. In 1969, he had received his Industrial Engineer College degree and had begun working at Eaton Corporation in Marshall, Michigan as the foreman. He had only been employed for three months when he was drafted to fight in the Vietnam War. Bill traveled to Kentucky and Oklahoma for training, but his orders were abruptly changed, and he was sent to Korea instead of Vietnam to work on assembling atomic bombs. His plan was to return to Eaton and continue his education when he finished his duty in the army.

Although Bill was 23 and I was 26, I felt that he was mature from all of his life experiences. He was easy to talk to, and we began to exchange facts about our lives. As time went on, I liked him more and more because he seemed sincere and genuine. Bill started to come see me more at work whenever he had a chance and would show me letters he exchanged with his mom after he told her about me. One day he offered to take me out on the town. Other men had asked me out in the past too, but I had always declined because I was not ready for a relationship. I had seen too many men, especially my dad, who did not respect women. The women that were part of the other married couples around me were suffering because many Korean men were untruthful hypocrites and cheating on their wives. I promised myself that I would never allow that to happen to me. But then my only friend Un, quit her job, and got married to a U.S. Soldier. She was very happy and told me that I should also quit my job and get married before it was too late. It made me rethink and reconsider. I also reminded myself that there were many good and honest men too, like my uncles.

In the end I was greatly influenced by my friend Un. I initially declined Bill's offers to go out, but after three months I finally agreed. I no longer had anyone to talk to because my one and only friend, Un, got married and she spent most of her time with her husband. I started feeling lonely. I had every third Sunday off, so Bill and I discussed what we would do. We had another problem to solve, because we had to figure out a meeting place where no one could see us. So we had to travel to a different city because I was not legally permitted to date an American G.I. while working on the U.S. military base. We took a taxi and went to the next city and spent the entire day sitting in a tea shop in the back corner hiding. I sipped milk, while Bill drank coffee. I didn't drink coffee or tea back then. We each shared details about our respective families. Since I wasn't supposed to date G.I.s, I was concerned about how things would work out for me if I dated Bill. I had no idea what Bill was contemplating. What was it that he liked about me, and did he want to take me with him to the U.S.? I wondered if he felt sorry for me after he heard the story of my life. I suddenly questioned his interest in me. Did he see that my character was bold, truthful, and hard-working? Then Bill visited me at work a week or so later and asked, "Can we do that again?" He said he had a good time with me. Because I wasn't allowed to socialize with G.I.s, I was still nervous. Bill recommended that we try moving further away. He claimed he had never toured Seoul and thought that going there would be fun. We decided to take a taxi to Seoul for a day trip and explored the entire city. We went to historical locations with lovely old palaces and parks.

We continued escaping to Seoul a few more times, twice with my brother and once with my friend Un. These trips helped us get to know one another better, and I grew to appreciate him more. I shared my family situation and lack of education with Bill who told me that would not be an issue in the U.S. He said I could finish high school and go to college any time. Bill appeared understanding of my family's circumstances and said he might be able to help. He claimed he intended to take me to America. Even though I liked Bill, I still didn't take what he said too seriously. At the time, my plan was still to start some kind of business in Korea to support my family.

Bill clearly cared deeply about his family, as seen by the frequency of his mother's letters. He had an air of responsibility about him. He began sharing his mother's letters with me. After Bill told his parents about me, his mother Jean began sending me letters with pictures. I soon found out about Bill's Grandma Barnes, a widow who lived alone and was the mother of Bill's dad. I grew more confident in Bill as I learned that Grandma Barnes, his maternal grandparents, and the rest of his family were devout Christians. Additionally, he had a brother named Mark who was 5 years younger serving in the Navy. His sister, who was two years older, tragically passed away at the age of 18 in a car accident. He seemed melancholy when he recalled his sister because they had been close.

Bill liked watching James Bond films and took me to see a few of them including *Gone with the Wind*, which I liked so much that I watched it multiple times. Going to movies made me feel like I knew a little more about America. After his work shift, Bill would stop by my apartment which I shared with my three brothers. I never had a lot of free time because I had to clean and do laundry. When he came over, I would make ramen noodles, Bill's favorite food for us to eat. My brothers loved his jokes and the small gifts he would bring them, such as pieces of chocolate. He would even occasionally visit them when I wasn't home.

Bill continued to tell me about America. I didn't have a map but I knew that it was a big country with a lot of opportunities. Korea is a small nation (roughly the size of Indiana or Portugal or Hungary) and I had only visited a few places outside my area of employment. He showed me a picture of his family's farmhouse and talked to me about Michigan, including the weather there. Bill's family also owned homes in Florida and Canada, where they kept cabins for hunting and fishing. I was amazed that one family could own three homes, and I assumed that America must be an extremely wealthy nation.

My thoughts towards marriage began to change as my life objectives shifted. We started to discuss our future. I would have to make a decision quickly because Bill would be done with the military in a few months. I agreed to marry him, and our engagement was now official. I first gave notice to my work, and told them my plan to marry an American soldier. They wished me good luck!

After a month I quit working. I felt relieved but I also realized how much my life would change. We applied for a marriage license, but corrupt government workers kept delaying our marriage documents for no reason, and kept asking us for additional money for the paperwork. I didn't want to pay them, and I hated that Korean people expected bribes for everything. Back then, if you needed to get something done and fast, whether legal or not, you had to pay a bribe. I couldn't begin applying for a visa and my background check until I had my marriage license. Bill took my friend Un, my brother Heung-Gu, and me to Seoul a couple more times while we were waiting for our marriage license. Meanwhile, I found it difficult to comprehend how much had happened in a single year.

On June 9, 1971, Bill and I were finally wed at the American Embassy in Seoul in front of one of the American officials who witnessed our marriage vows, and signed the marriage papers. We hurried back to the military installation so he could complete his work before departing. Bill was supposed to leave for the U.S. a few days after we got married. Our plan was to go to the U.S. together, but my marriage papers were delayed. Although I found out too late, the majority of Korean government employees working for the American Embassy were corrupt and dishonest, and I was forced to stay behind to wait for my visa while Bill traveled back home alone. Bill wanted to take all my belongings that I planned to bring with me to America, including my clothing. He said this would be significantly less expensive compared to exporting them. After Bill was gone, I felt lost. I was so lonely, and I didn't have anyone close to talk to. For the first time in my life, I had a lot of time on my hands but I was not able to enjoy it. I couldn't eat, read, sleep, or shop, as I felt very depressed. I soon realized I had never really had the chance to develop deep personal relationships with anyone. I only had my family and work.

My major objective after Bill left was to obtain my visa. I would ride the bus and walk for hours to the American embassy in Seoul every week to ask about the status. I was initially assured that it would just take a month at most. But every time I went, I never got a guarantee that it would be done. I started to worry. One day while standing in another long line at the embassy, a man in front of me informed me that I would have to give extra money to the embassy employees in order to obtain my visa. I came to understand that the majority of government employees were corrupt, and they purposely caused delays in order to solicit bribes. Although it was an American Embassy, almost all the employees were Korean in order for them to easily communicate with other Koreans. Unfortunately, those Korean Embassy staff abused their power and took advantage of people. I hated going there as they were so arrogant. I remember that they always looked at us contemptuously and were never friendly. Even though it was their job, they treated us like they were doing us a favor. I felt they especially disliked women who were married to American soldiers. As soon as they saw my new married last name, they would look down and ignore me. The Embassy employees had seen my records, so they knew I didn't have any connection to higher government authorities. They also knew how desperately I wanted to leave the country. Other women who were in a desperate state like me paid the bribe without hesitation. I knew they wanted more bribes from me, but I didn't want to give them any more and thought I could wait it out. I went to the American Embassy every week for three months. Sometimes when I was waiting in the long line to inquire about my visa status, I would see one or two Americans, but it seemed like they didn't know what was going on in the embassy. They would come out of an office, stand in the back of the room, look around but never talked to anyone then retreated back to their room. Meanwhile, four or five Korean women and men were busy running around, whispering. In my mind I thought they were busy creating false documents, or trying to cover up something they did together. The Americans appeared so naive, and it was obvious they didn't realize that the Koreans were demanding bribes right under their noses.

Since I was no longer employed on the army installation, I didn't have access to a phone. I wanted to call Bill to let him know about the circumstances and ask for his opinion. The majority of Koreans at the time lacked a phone that could make international calls. I made the decision to stop paying extra money because I knew they would keep requesting more and more. This would go on indefinitely unless I did something to stop it. There was no use for looking for a job, since I would have to resign as soon as my visa arrived.

The only thing I could do was pray and read the Bible while I waited. I used to work on the base on Sundays, which prevented me from going to church. I decided to go to a church to pray, since I no longer worked, but was uncomfortable introducing myself to people because my situation was just temporary.

Months passed and I still didn't have my visa. I wanted to give my mother what little money I had before I left Korea, but I didn't want to go back to the village and answer all the questions from the nosey neighbors and families. In our village everyone was involved in each other's business. Dad was my only visitor, and he always demanded cash from me, while assuring me that he would deliver it to my mother. I later learned that Dad had not given her any money, and he didn't even return home right away. I was furious with him. How could I ever trust him again?

I reached out to my friend Un in Los Angeles and wrote a letter to her explaining my predicament. She told me that she had a bad experience with the American Embassy too. She also told me she had enrolled in a beauty school because she had grown lonely since her husband had been sent back to Vietnam. She told me that life in the U.S. was not easy.

Bill and I only had a few opportunities to speak over the phone. I missed him a lot, and we wrote letters to one another frequently. Hearing that he was making plans made me optimistic, but I was unsure if they would be fulfilled. I thought about many things and wondered how my family would manage without me, so I could not sleep at night. Having no appetite, I went from 93 pounds to under 85 pounds. Finally, I learned that my visa would be approved. I was so relieved! Three months of waiting felt incredibly long and more like 3 years. Without a question, this was the loneliest time of my life.

Children

Bill & Moon-Hea

Bill & Song-Hea in Pool

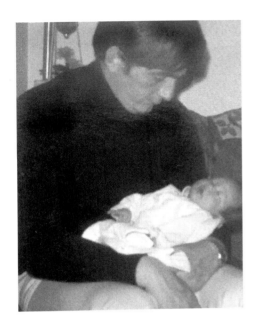

Bill & Yong-Hea

Sue & Moon-Hea

93

Sue & Song-Hea

Sue & Yong-Hea

94

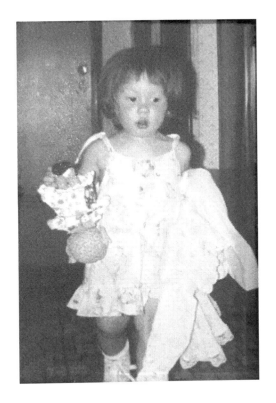

Yong-Hea with doll

Yong-Hea playing piano

Yong-Hea Violin Lessons

Yong-Hea recital

Moon-Hea, Bill & Song-Hea

Bill & Song-Hea

97

Grandpa & Moon-Hea

Song-Hea, Yong-Hea & Moon-Hea

Piano lessons Song-Hea & Moon-Hea

99

Performing for family

Moon-Hea & Song-Hea

Song-Hea after solo Kalamazoo Symphony

Moon-Hea, Yong-Hea & Song-Hea

Grandchildren

All six grandchildren

Josef, Bill & Alex

Lucas, Moses & Mena

Mena & Sue

Lee Family

My Father

Seok-Gu & Hong-Gu

Jeong-Gu, Karen, Tae-Gu, Song-Hee, Mom & Heung-Gu

109

Family camping in the West

Sackrider Family

Bill & Sue in Korea

Bill & Sue in Africa

Bill & Sue Florida

Bill, Josef, Song-Hea & Jean

Sue talking to Girl Scouts about Korea
two weeks after arrival

Family

Chapter 12
Early Life in America

The time had finally come for me to go to America. I called Bill one last time to give him my itinerary. As I prepared for my first plane ride, I contemplated what the experience might be like. Heung-Gu came to the airport to see me off. I told him to stay in school, and that I would do my best to send money when I could. I felt so sorry for him that I gave him another $50 even though I had already given him money earlier. We hugged and cried when we had to say good-bye to each other. The security personnel at the Korean airport were also arrogant and corrupt, and they demanded an additional $50 from me when I checked in, claiming my papers were incorrect and that they had to fix them. I didn't even question it because I knew they were making up a story. I just wanted to leave this worthless country as quickly as possible. I reluctantly gave them my last $50 bill, which left me with only $20. The plane was six hours late but I never learned why. Finally, I boarded my flight to America. I had a lot of time to think about my situation, and I realized that I only had $20 dollars in my pocket. I was truly helpless and possibly stupid. I just trusted that Bill told me the truth. "When you get off the plane, I will be right there waiting for you! Don't worry about bringing any money, I will take care of you from now on. All you need is money to get to the United States." Was I irresponsible and incredibly naive? Even now, when I look back on that decision, I was not very wise. On the airplane, I couldn't stop thinking about my future in America. What kind of life could I expect in America? Would I have a hard time? How would my marriage be? I also reflected on how Korea was such a corrupt country that I never want to come back, but how would my family survive?

Our flight had to stop in Japan first, then finally landed in Seattle, Washington, for immigration formalities. Compared to airports in Korea, this one was much bigger. Knowing where to go was very confusing, so I tried to follow other people around. I only knew I wasn't in Los Angeles yet. A kind older gentleman noticed I was lost and told me to follow him down a long hallway to where I needed to be. He went out of his way to assist me. I was struck by how different the Americans I encountered were from the Koreans at the embassy, even the Americans working at the airport. Nobody asked me for money and everyone seemed friendly.

After a long screening time in Seattle, I boarded another airplane that took me to Los Angeles. Once again, I didn't know what to do when the plane landed. I had just come from the airport in Seattle and thought that was big, but LAX was like a city of its own! I was in disbelief. Some nice women tried to help me at LAX, and the people there were courteous but I was still unable to locate Bill. He was nowhere to be found, which wasn't what we had planned. I called my Los Angeles-based friend Un, and she arrived with her mother-in-law. Even though I was overjoyed to see them, I was still worried because I couldn't find Bill. (Remember none of us had cell phones in those days.) We searched for him in the airport for a couple of hours but because my plane had been delayed by six hours, Bill was also having a hard time finding me. I was finally able to reach Jean, Bill's mother, thanks to Un's mother-in-law. She let me know that Bill had left for LAX four days earlier. After wandering around the airport for some time, I finally spoke with an employee who suggested that we page him.

When we arrived at the meeting location, Bill was already there waiting. I was overjoyed to see him. He had grown his hair out a little and he had gained some weight. I assumed that his mother was spoiling him with home cooked meals. Bill grabbed me and gave me a long, strong hug while he took note of how thin I was. We were happy to be together at last.

The next day, Bill said he would take me to Disneyland. Un's mother-in-law invited us over, so we stopped by their house first. I had no idea what to expect in America, and I was mesmerized during the drive. I had never seen 5-lane highways filled with shiny, colorful automobiles and so many tall buildings. The tropical trees, flowers, and lush vegetation also surprised me. In Korea, the buildings were small and damaged, and most of the trees were destroyed or were cut down to be used for heating, cooking, and constructing different products.

Un's mother-in-law lived in a ranch-style home that was much larger than I was used to. I saw a washing machine and a stove for the first time. Bill was excited to show me I would no longer need to do laundry by hand. After our visit, Bill and I checked into a Ramada hotel that was modest but was still wonderful to me. The next day we left for Disneyland. Bill was tense driving in the congested Los Angeles traffic but we eventually arrived. We spent all day at the park, and I thought it was fantastic. "The Hall of Presidents" was my favorite exhibit. I learned about the history of the United States and watched audio-animatronic representations of each president. I reflected on how different my own country Korea was to this amazing country.

From there, we made stops at many different locations, including Death Valley in the Mojave Desert, Las Vegas in Nevada, the Arizona desert, the Grand Canyon, and the Rocky Mountains. I was astounded that such diverse landscapes could exist in one nation. Each location had a unique landscape. Dazzlingly colored sands and rocks, cacti of all sizes, stunning mountains, vast swaths of lush vegetation, and sparkling rivers. Every place we visited was incredible to me. Bill had never visited these areas before either. I couldn't stop saying, "Oh wow! Wow!"

We saw a lot of young people in California, both men and women, with long, uncombed hair and bangs, loose clothing, and cowboy boots. (In Korean cities, men wore suits and dressed formally. Koreans still dress this way now. People there tend to place more value on appearance.) Bill explained to me they were "hippies." When we stopped at a gas station a young couple approached Bill and asked if they could catch a ride with us. I was surprised when he agreed. Bill's Mustang was small and we already had three suitcases of our own, yet somehow we all managed to cram inside. There was no air conditioning, and it was still quite hot in early September. While we were traveling through the desert, neither Bill nor I said a word to the strangers. They talked quietly to one another while huddled together in the back seat. They seemed like a decent couple, but I felt uneasy nonetheless. After almost a day of traveling together, we dropped them off somewhere in Arizona. When I shared this story later with a few friends, they all made jokes about how fortunate we were not to have been kidnapped. Honestly, I believe that people back then were more trustworthy than they are today.

There were many different restaurants in America, but I didn't see any serving Korean food, and I didn't want to bother searching for one. Bill always chose hamburgers for every meal. He told me it was his favorite dish and that he had survived solely on hamburgers during his time in college. I had a poor appetite and no knowledge of American cuisine, other than hamburgers, steak, fried chicken, and sandwiches. I didn't want to eat much even though I was hungry. I'd carry a bucket of Kentucky Fried Chicken around with me to nibble on throughout the day. Fried chicken was considered a luxury food in Korea but now Korean fried chicken is very popular in America.

After our sightseeing tour out west, we started heading toward Michigan. However, first we had to travel through Kansas, Missouri, Illinois, Indiana, and Ohio. I was still baffled as to how such a large country could exist. On this final leg of our journey, the scenery looked remarkably different and started to flatten out. There were no longer beautiful mountains or an abundance of large trees - for a long time we only saw farmland and cows, and it started getting colder. We were anxious to get to Michigan, so we didn't make any stops except for food and gas for the final three days. I kept asking, "Bill, will the driving ever end? When will we arrive at your house?" Every time, with a smile, he would respond, "It'll be very soon, just a few more hours."

We finally arrived in Michigan the last week of September. Bill pulled off the freeway, and we headed down a backroad. As we continued, we saw a few far-flung farmhouses until we came to a remote farm with a long dirt driveway. I was taken aback when Bill revealed that this was his home. I questioned how anybody could live without neighbors nearby. In Korea, people lived in close proximity to each other, even on farms in the countryside. They collaborated in the fields, shared a public well, looked out for one another, and engaged in social activities. I immediately saw that I would struggle to understand this new culture.

Bill's parents were scheduled to get home from work shortly after we arrived. He gave me a tour of their home which had three bedrooms, one bathroom, a living room, kitchen, dining room, and laundry area. I was impressed because it was much larger than our home in Korea. Meeting Bill's parents made me uncomfortable and a little nervous, but it quickly became clear that they were wonderful people.

In Korean culture, it is improper to address adults by their first names, so I called them Mom and Dad. I was so exhausted that I don't even recall the supper Jean prepared, only that the food was lovingly presented. After dinner, we said our good nights and went upstairs to our bedroom, where we jammed two twin beds together. There was no insulation or heat, but since I was used to being cold, it wasn't a problem for me.

Two weeks later, Jean and Frank hosted a lovely wedding reception celebration for us at their Methodist church. I met all of his extended family (grandparents, uncles, aunts, and cousins) and made a lot of new friends. I was surprised to see that the men were working in the kitchen and wearing aprons.

Meanwhile, the women were all dressed up beautifully, setting up decorations and placing gifts for us on tables. Others were greeting guests in the dining room while visiting and talking to each other. Later I found out that one of the men owned a large turkey farm and restaurant. I'm sure they were very busy people, but at our wedding reception, they were humble and happy to serve in the kitchen. All of this was so different from Korea where the women do all the work in the kitchen and at home, serving the men and family. I'm not sure if this is the same now, but when I was growing up this was the custom mandated from the Yi Dynasty. A few weeks later, we visited Mackinac Island, where I recall feeling queasy on the boat but still had a nice trip.

Meeting people at reception

We continued to adjust to our new life. I stayed alone at the farmhouse while Bill and his parents went to work. In the evening, I helped Jean in the kitchen while she prepared dinner so I could learn how to cook American food. I still missed rice and Korean food but there was no place to buy Korean groceries. I found out later that when Jean found out we were getting married, she had searched the Battle Creek area to find Korean friends for me. I have always been grateful to her for introducing me to Sandy and Heaja. Sandy was really helpful because she had lived in the U.S. for seven years. They would order ingredients from Korea, and we would prepare food at their houses. Our friendship enabled our husbands to get to know each other, and we all enjoyed spending time together. Jean ended up being the only one in Bill's family who liked kimchi and rice!

When I wasn't able to visit my friends, there were only cats, chickens, pigs, and a lot of pine trees to interact with on the 80-acre farm. There wasn't one other person to talk to. I thought it was a big farm but Bill told me that it was small compared to some others in the area. His dad Frank worked at Kellogg's, the cereal company, and this farm was just his hobby. I started to get really bored and lonely when they all went to work. I read some books to pass the time, but it didn't help much. My Korean friends lived too far away for me to visit their homes, and I had to wait for Bill to teach me how to drive. While Bill's family and church friends were kind and tried to help me adapt to my new life, I still felt alone and stuck. My English was so poor that I was afraid to say much.

Reception cake

When I worked on the military base in Korea, my English was very basic and broken. But since I could communicate and be understood, I thought my English was okay. Of course I knew I had to improve, but when people tried to engage in a conversation or joke with me here in America, I had a hard time understanding. I realized the language and culture were so different; every gesture could easily be misinterpreted. I had to be cautious about what I said so as not to make everyone laugh. I thought about a lot of things. How could I ever learn western customs? I couldn't understand the relationship between parents and children, friendships, and the food culture.

Everyone I met seemed tall and good looking compared to me. I felt like a girl from a poor country who didn't know anything. I started feeling depressed due to my inferiority complex. I tried to explain my feelings to Bill, but he didn't seem to understand. He'd brush my comments aside and say, "But you are beautiful and will learn everything soon. I love you, and I will help you."

One day I started to feel ill and constantly queasy, throwing up every day. I thought these symptoms were a result of everything I had gone through or perhaps all the new food I had been trying that didn't agree with me. I hoped the illness would go away on its own, but Bill brought me to the doctor after it became worse. He looked me over and asked if it was possible I was pregnant. I told him I still had my period so I didn't think so. The doctor referred me to an ear, nose, and throat specialist because I had throat pain too, and I was advised to get my tonsils removed. But after my surgery, I got worse and had to spend over a month in the hospital. I went back down to 80 pounds after having gained some weight since my move to America. I was unable to swallow anything due to my sore throat, and the doctor gave me a variety of painkillers and antibiotics. Nothing seemed to work, and I was only upsetting my stomach more due to all the medications I was taking. The doctor then prescribed chewing gum containing aspirin (Aspergum) which made no difference at all.

I was unable to eat or sleep because I was in constant discomfort and thought I was going to die. Bill and his family heeded the advice of the medical professionals. They believed that we should wait and that I would eventually get better. In hindsight, I realize we were being naive. The family doctor continued to be involved, and after three months he finally gave me a pregnancy test. He never told me directly but then informed Bill that I was three months pregnant. I was in shock and felt so foolish and ashamed. I was also concerned about our unborn baby, but the doctor said the baby appeared to be in good health. Looking back now, I can clearly see how negligent the doctor was in my diagnosis. General anesthesia had been used during an unnecessary procedure that could have harmed my unborn child. I had taken many different ineffective drugs throughout my first trimester. I was still really sick when I got home from the hospital. I felt awful since my throat wasn't getting any better but there was nothing more I could do. I was only able to ask God for a healthy baby.

We settled into a rhythm at home. Every night Bill and his dad would watch TV on the couch while enjoying a bowl of popcorn. Jean taught me how to knit and crochet. I started knitting day and night to fill this monotonous period of waiting and to help me forget about my painful throat from the recent procedures. I made four men's sweaters and three shawls for the family as Christmas gifts. While knitting was in some ways my lifesaver, this was not what I had in mind when I came to America. I felt trapped and miserable because I was still sick and unable to move around. I wanted to travel and see more of this country. I wanted to attend school and learn how to drive. I was quite uncomfortable as my stomach grew bigger every day, but I tried to be positive and patient. As I began to feel depressed again, I started to wrongly believe I was stupid and helpless. There were many aspects of my body that I disliked, and I felt unattractive. I was finding it challenging to adapt to the culture here.

Bill's apparent inability to comprehend what I was going through irritated me. I asked him to take me somewhere and show me something new. He expressed concern for me, yet he was quiet. I realized now this was the reality of my married life in America. I was frustrated trying to adapt to this strange and unfamiliar environment. What new hurdles would I have to jump over? My biggest dilemma was trying to express my feelings to Bill with my limited English. I was overwhelmed and continued to nag him. We both came to the realization that we were very different from each other, and he also began to understand that marriage was not easy. I gained a fresh perspective on my own mother and how difficult her life had been. To his credit, Bill was a decent and hard-working man who didn't drink excessively or gamble like my father, and he came home every day after work. My life was not nearly as tough as my mom's, but I still felt like I had little control over my circumstances. However, I had chosen this life; therefore, I told myself to carry on no matter what happened. Whenever I was down, I would call, "Oh! God! Help me!" again and again. "God! I need Your Help!" was my prayer. Because God knows me, and He knows my heart. I'm still doing this prayer. Whenever I'm down, it works for me every time.

Bill tried to teach me how to drive with his Mustang, but I couldn't even reach the pedals. This was a sports car with bucket seats and a stick shift, not an automatic transmission. When we were dating in Korea, he had told me that driving would be so simple that I would be able to operate the steering wheel with one finger. I told him, "You lied to me!" He said he'd just been joking when he'd said that.

In the end, Bill was able to use his mother's car to teach me how to drive. I practiced driving with everyone in the family. Mom, Dad, and Bill all helped me learn to drive. I was five or six months pregnant. Eventually I received my driver's license. In order for me to drive our car, Bill paid more money to exchange his Mustang for a car with automatic transmission. I was impatient for us to have our own home since I didn't want to be left alone in the countryside with a baby after everyone else went to work. I kept nagging Bill to get an apartment closer to the city. After a lot of arguing, Bill reluctantly took me on a search for a new home but told me that he preferred to buy a house rather than rent. I was seven months pregnant at this point.

Jean and Frank thought this was a great idea and went with us to look for a house. I am sure that six months of living together was enough for them too. However, we didn't have the money for a down payment and would still need to purchase furniture and other items for the new home. Bill and his father spoke with Grandma Barnes who loaned us $2,000 for a down payment so that we could buy the house. We agreed to monthly payments for two years at the same interest rate she received from her bank. We paid $19,000 for a three-bedroom ranch house in Marshall that was about five minutes from Bill's workplace.

We moved in and quickly got to fixing up the house, starting with the nursery. Jean's father, Grandpa Smith, made a wooden highchair. Jean and Frank brought us baby supplies nearly every day. It was a scorching summer, but everyone was excited and busy preparing for the baby. We didn't know if it was a boy or a girl. I asked Bill and Jean to come up with a nice American name, but they were at a loss. Bill suggested we think about a Korean name. Korean names for girls are often unique and special, so Bill asked me to choose a Korean name. When our first daughter was born on July 30, 1972, I named her Moon-Hea after my friend I grew up with in Korea as I always liked her name. We chose her middle name as Susan, after Bill's older sister Suzanne who passed away when Bill was in high school.

She was a 7-pound baby girl who thankfully was in excellent health. We were so happy and grateful for our little baby girl with such a pretty face. Her appearance favored both sides of our family.

After Moon-Hea was born, my illness disappeared. I had a brand new sense of self. I thought it was a miracle that I had been cured of my difficult nine months of suffering. I felt incredibly grateful for God's grace toward me and our daughter. Later I learned that if any part of your body gets cut or if you catch the flu or cold during your pregnancy, it usually will not get better or heal until you deliver. Even though I had assisted my mom in raising my brothers, I still felt unprepared to take care of my own child. I wanted to learn everything I could about babies, and do things the right way. But Jean didn't say much about what to do with Moon-Hea. I presume she wanted to avoid becoming an overbearing mother-in-law. After about four months of breastfeeding, my milk started to run out, so I switched to bottle feeding.

As time went on, I got to know more people. It seemed like I was finally moving towards my goals. I was getting to know my neighbors who made me feel more at ease, and I was gaining more confidence. Our neighbors Martha and Kay became good friends, and they were also good seamstresses. They taught me all kinds of sewing techniques, which was so fun for me to learn. Bill bought me a new Viking sewing machine for about $500, which was very expensive for that time. I started making all kinds of clothes for me, the baby, and even a leisure suit for Bill and his father. I immersed myself in daily housework, sewing constantly, even making my own pants and dresses. I also made curtains, sewed baby outfits, and prepared meals using new American recipes. I became a competent homemaker, mother, and wife, with sewing, cooking, and gardening occupying my free time.

I soon realized that learning English was the first step in achieving my educational goals. My English had improved slightly since moving to America, but it was still discouraging that I wasn't picking it up as quickly as I would have liked. I began to think that maybe Koreans were pitiful in comparison to Americans because my Korean acquaintances experienced the same issue learning the new language. Though I wasn't as depressed as I had been, it was difficult to keep from comparing myself to Americans. I was aware that everyone is unique but I couldn't help feeling self-conscious. Americans appeared to be much taller and more attractive. Perhaps culture shock was starting to affect me, but I was determined to keep moving forward and to keep fighting.

I was very busy doing projects all the time, but I enrolled in a night class called "English as a Second Language" so that Bill could watch Moon-Hea during the evenings. Four students from Vietnam, Mexico, and Eastern Europe were also enrolled. During class we just spent time trying to have conversations with each other in English. I attended this class for an entire year but it didn't improve my English as much as I had hoped.

I was also always looking for work to make money to help my family in Korea. Bill's income was just enough to pay our bills and to pay back Grandma Barnes' loan. There weren't a lot of job opportunities in the small town we lived in and I also had a small baby. I was finally able to find work at a factory close to our home. They produced nuts and bolts for cars but I was forced to leave after about three months due to concerns with our babysitter. Moon-Hea was only six months old at the time. I was able to send my family $1,000 which was every penny I earned during those three months.

Bill still struggled to comprehend how I was feeling. He would go to work, then come home and usually watch TV to unwind. Bill seemed content but I didn't feel the same way. When Moon-Hea was one year old, Bill started working on his Master's degree at Western Michigan University, an hour away from home. For two years, he attended classes three times a week after work. I was happy that Bill wanted to get more education, and I really wanted to encourage him as much as I could even though I want to start my education too, so I let him go first. I started feeling stuck and bored as I cared for our precious baby girl in the evening alone. Bill usually didn't get home until almost midnight, and then he had to be at work at 8 in the morning, so he was gone for most of the day. I kept telling myself that life in America was far better than back home in Korea, so what was I complaining about? I realized I had to get over my self-pity and persist in making every effort to become a better person. I thought to myself it will be better soon. I encouraged myself to express gratitude for my improved health. Little Moon-Hea was thriving and in good health, and we had moved into our own home.

Meanwhile in the back of my mind I couldn't help worrying about my family in Korea. I believed that God had given me the duty to keep looking after them. I sent them letters and photos in addition to what little money I could. They assumed we were wealthy based on the photos. Dad continued to drink and gamble, but they noted in their letters that he wasn't as bad as he had been, as my younger two brothers grew older and bigger. Jeong-Gu and Tae-Gu were popular and excelled at sports. They both played soccer well and continued to study Tae Kwon Do. My sister Song-Hea was twenty years younger than me so I hadn't spent a lot of time with her because she was born after I moved out of the house, but I always loved all my siblings. I still wanted to do everything I could to help them.

After I left for America, I didn't hear much about Heung-Gu. Seok-Gu later told me that he had a tough time and couldn't finish high school because my family didn't have the money. He was then called to join the Korean army for the required military service. I thought about what I should do to help them have a better life. I still had my own personal difficulties in this new country, while trying to quickly learn so many things.

When Moon-Hea was two years old, I became pregnant with our second child. Although I was sick again throughout this pregnancy, I was more prepared due to what I'd learned in my first pregnancy. I knew I had to accept things as they were. I went back to attending the same evening English classes for one more year. After that, I enrolled in the local high school to complete my high school education. Our cherished second daughter Song-Hea Kim was born on October 9, 1974.

Chapter 13

My Family in Korea Joins Us

After three years, I was able to obtain my citizenship and I asked Bill if it would be possible to bring a couple of my brothers to America. He agreed that we could try. Soon afterwards we started the process but I was in for a shock. Legally, my father had to come over first, because my brothers who were 16 and 18 were supposedly under my father's guardianship. I thought, "No way, God! I don't want to bring my father here to my new life. How in the world could this be happening to me? Lord, are You punishing me for something I did wrong?" At first I could not even consider this because I was done with him. I knew for sure that my Dad would never change his lifestyle, and I would never go back to my old life and put up with his behavior. I wanted to bring my brothers to the U.S. first, and after they got settled in, I would try to bring my mother and sister. In my mind, Dad could live wherever he wanted to in

Korea as he did throughout my life, and I simply wanted him to leave us alone. I felt he was the main cause of all the misery in our family's life. He never once apologized or took responsibility for anything. I contemplated this impossible situation often, trying to figure out how I could only bring my mom and siblings.

I was aware that conditions in Korea were still bad, and poverty persisted as few jobs were available. The lack of work only led people to act badly. People become dissatisfied and aimless when they don't have work or an income. My father had led a life that I didn't want my brothers to follow; this was very important for me. Unsure of their situation, I wanted to see them face to face, so I decided I needed to visit them in Korea.

I made the decision to travel to Korea with Moon-Hea in 1975 when she was three years old, and Song-Hea was nine months old. It was a difficult trip from beginning to end. We flew from Chicago to Los Angeles, but our initial Korean airlines flight was postponed because it was overbooked. We had to stay overnight to wait for the next flight in the same LAX airport I'd wandered around in looking for Bill when I'd first come to America. Moon-Hea needed some time to settle down once we boarded for the lengthy 14-hour flight. When we arrived in Korea, five or six of my extended family, including my dad, were waiting in the airport. We eventually made it to my family's home again via train and bus. Grandma was extremely frail and almost blind. Her eyes had started getting bad while I was working in Korea, and I remember taking her to the doctor to check her eyes. But he had told me that she had glaucoma and her case was not treatable. She was unable to see us, but when she heard my voice, she patted me and Moon-Hea with her hands. I was happy to see everyone, but I was very sad about

Grandma's situation. We often cried together. Moon-Hea and I slept with Grandma.

My brother Seok-Gu was now 29 years old and had returned home after serving in Vietnam. My sister Song-Hee, whom I knew very little of, was just 10 years old. My brothers Jeong-Gu (18) and Tae-Gu (16) were still in high school. I didn't get to see Heung-Gu during that trip since he was serving in the military, which was mandatory for all male Korean citizens between the ages of 18 and 28.

Even though my father's behavior was slightly better, my family's situation still felt dismal. I knew then that I couldn't give up, even if it meant having to put up with my father. I was adamant that I would continue my plans to bring my siblings and mother to America. But in order to immigrate to America, my family had to overcome significant challenges. Korean public servants were still dishonest and demanded bribes. We were also worried that Tae-Gu and Jeong-Gu would be called to finish their mandatory Korean military service. In addition, the cost of the airplane tickets would be very expensive. I advised my parents to put their home and any other assets up for sale and told my brothers to organize their affairs and gather the required documents.

In the meantime, I regretted my decision to bring Moon-Hea to Korea. We traveled in August, a month that was extremely hot and humid, because the tickets were more affordable. We were accustomed to having a refrigerator and air conditioning in America, but no matter where we went in Korea, the heat never seemed to let up. Little Moon-Hea didn't know my family, so she was frightened when she met them. She was visited by every neighbor in the area, but she clung to me and didn't want to interact with any of them. She was probably experiencing culture shock because the setting was so different. I was exhausted from the flight, and we both had diarrhea from the water even though we had medication from the American doctor to use in case we got sick. I'd brought peanut butter, but Moon-Hea wasn't happy eating this for every meal. I used a safety leash with her in the airport and everywhere I went in Seoul, because I was terrified of losing her in the crowds.

One day, I needed to exchange money at the bank, so I left Moon-Hea with my brothers for about twenty minutes at a tea house. When I returned, they told me that she had kicked and screamed the entire time I was gone. I couldn't even use the restroom by myself after that. On that trip, Moon-Hea underwent a lot of trauma and suffered as a result of my family issues and my poor judgment in bringing her. Song-Hea, whom I had left in Michigan with Bill, Jean, Grandma Barnes, and my neighbor Martha, was also continually on my mind.

A month later, Moon-Hea and I were ready to come back home and slept the entire way. When we'd initially purchased our tickets on Korean Airlines, there had been a special offer and lower pricing for those who planned to stay a full month. Now I wished I had stayed for only two weeks. After our plane touched down in Los Angeles, we changed to American Airlines and flew to Chicago. When Bill met us at the airport, he said we both looked half dead. I was eagerly looking forward to holding Song-Hea in my arms as we traveled to Michigan, but I'll never forget my daughter's dejected expression when she first saw me. She looked so sad, began to sob and turned back to Bill. She appeared to be saying, "I don't know you! Who are you?" Song-Hea didn't come to me right away, but when she finally did, she still looked sad and like she wanted to cry. Eventually she seemed to recognize my voice and then approached me voluntarily and gave me a hug sobbing. That moment of my child's hurting and sad expression is engraved in my heart forever. Because God put those feelings in all the mothers' hearts. (Isaiah 49:15) "Can a mother forget the baby at her breast and have no compassion for the child she has borne? Though she may forget, I will not forget you!" ('Lord! Thank you so much for your amazing promise to us!' I'm so grateful and You will never leave me no matter what happens").

I felt bad about what I made my kids go through for my family. However, every one of my three daughters grew up to be uncontrollable teenagers and slowly turned into strangers who didn't like anything I did and looked down on me. I didn't really understand their problems. I'm sure that there was some misunderstanding due to culture and language too, however, when I was hurt by my husband and our children, I tried to remember the good memories I had from when they were young, and it always helped me have a softer and generous heart. God is very wise.

Once I got back to America, we started working hard to get ready for my family's arrival. Bill and I purchased a larger house further out in the country, since we didn't have enough space in our home for everyone. I was also worried about my dad drinking and making a scene with neighbors close by. My parents sold their house and possessions in the interim, but they accepted a neighbor's exceedingly low offer as everyone knew they were leaving for America. In those days it was a very big thing for the whole family to immigrate to America. They believed we were very wealthy, so everyone tried to take advantage of them.

The plan was to bring my younger siblings first so they could attend school here in the U.S. My parents, along with my sister Song-Hee who was eleven years old at the time, took a flight to America first. They were probably allowed to leave the country because they were old and would not significantly contribute to the country's economy. Seok-Gu arrived three months later because he had already served his military obligation in the Vietnam War. Heung-Gu was doing his mandatory military service. My two younger brothers, on the other hand, were interrogated by the Korean employees at the American Embassy several times and for some reason they were not approved for their visas. They were in the same situation as I was, indefinitely waiting without knowing the reason why their visas were not approved.

It was traumatic for Jeong-Gu and Tae-Gu to be in limbo. The Korean officials at the American Embassy made up false stories to obtain more bribes before they could travel to the United States. They claimed that Tae-Gu was not my parents' son. This was absurd. I helped Mom raise Tae-Gu since he was born and for many years before I left home. Until we could find a workable solution, they were left to find an apartment on their own in Korea, unable to complete high school and struggling to survive.

Although we anticipated a lot of paperwork, we felt that contacting the U.S. government would give us the best chance of getting my brothers to America. Bill's mother Jean wrote to Garry Brown, their U.S. House representative. Rep. Brown was able to get in touch with Henry Kissinger, who served as Nixon's national security adviser. A letter with Kissinger's signature was delivered to the American embassy in Korea. Bill and I took Mom and Dad to the Korean embassy in Detroit for blood tests a couple of times. It was a very hectic and long process to go through, but I learned that in the United States they didn't abuse their power. They followed a step-by-step process to ensure we were treated fairly, and that the resolution was based on the law. Tae-Gu's DNA analysis was done in Korea very quickly. I am sure the Koreans at the American Embassy were surprised and afraid that they had received a letter from White House, so they had no choice but to approve. This process took about three months, wasting a lot of our time, energy and money.

My family had to bribe and pay so many people to help them obtain their visas, that they ran out of money, even after borrowing money from uncles and aunts. They were forced to fly to America on credit with interest. I didn't even know that this was possible. I understand the Korean government must have been so desperate that they would do anything to improve their economy. It took about five to six years for my brothers to pay off the debt after they came to the U.S. I can't help but still feel cold and angry towards Korea because of these experiences. The Korean government did nothing to help me or my family. They only harassed and took money from us, until we finally left that country.

During this time I stopped going to the evening high school classes for a while because I needed to find work. We had purchased a bigger home with more land in order to have all of my family live with us. I worked as a waitress at the Fireside Inn restaurant in Marshall and the Riverside Country Club in Battle Creek. My mom and sister cared for Moon-Hea, who was 5 and Song-Hea who was 3, while I was at work. I would drive my brothers to English school between my work shifts. I also found dishwashing jobs for them at the restaurant. I thought they needed to do anything to learn English in America. So I drove them to work too. I finally gave my two brothers driving lessons, which was one of the hardest things I had to do.

In the beginning Dad was okay gardening a little and he seemed to enjoy working outside. But it wasn't long before he started to complain about how he was bored and wanted to visit Korea. He seemed to complain all the time while insisting he needed money or that he wanted to earn his own money. I discussed this with the restaurant owner and was able to secure Dad a job cleaning in the early morning. I saw this as a good opportunity for him to learn about American culture and help with his English-language skills. It ended up being a disaster. Dad was in his early 60s and had never cleaned anything in his life, so I had to spend extra time trying to teach him. I ended up working with him before my shift too.

Soon Bill and I felt completely overwhelmed by our predicament. Even though Bill had his own full-time job to focus on, he still helped me anyway he could. In my opinion, the "American Dream" is something frequently held up, yet it is by no means as simple as flipping a switch. Despite our making every effort to assist my family settle in America, they each faced challenges. Although getting to America was difficult, they thought that once they were here things would magically get better. They had no idea how challenging it would be to learn English and adjust to a new culture. While they faced these significant hurdles, I did everything I could to help them survive in this setting.

My family lived with us for two years. After six months, with Bill's help two of my brothers got a job at the Eaton factory making automobile parts so they were able to earn good money. They had to first pay off the debt they had accrued from buying their plane tickets. After that, they were able to save enough to make a down payment on a house that we helped them find. The entire family relocated to this new home in Marshall, and we all pitched in to help renovate it. Meanwhile, I got pregnant again. On February 17, 1977, we welcomed our third darling daughter, Yong-Hea, Sarah.

We believed that once my family owned their own home, they would be content. But after sharing a home for about four years, they struggled to get along. My sister Song-Hee was in middle school, and Tae-Gu was a high school student. Jeong-Gu attended Kellogg Community College at night while working at Eaton. When they had free time, Jeong-Gu and Tae-Gu continued their Tae Kwon Do practice. They had both earned their 3rd degree black belt in Korea, and wanted to become Tae Kwon Do masters and make a movie. They looked up to Bruce Lee, a well-known martial artist and Chinese movie star. I advised them to hold off from pursuing this dream and complete their college education so that they could obtain good jobs. I also suggested that they attend church so they could meet other Koreans. I wanted them to help support our parents, so I needed them to cooperate. My brothers were completely against my proposal. They told me they had not come to the United States to work in the manufacturing assembly line. Seok-Gu also had no desire to work in a factory. Still unmarried and lonely, he continued to spend his nights with other Koreans in Battle Creek, a city nearby. I knew my brothers felt discouraged and let down. I kept looking for opportunities to send my brothers to a bigger city because I thought Marshall was too small for them.

During my citizenship process, I met a Korean doctor, and he invited me to a Bible study in his family's home. I was impressed by the six couples that attended the lesson. We ate delicious Korean food and were joined by other Korean doctors. Bill and I had been going to the Methodist church in our community, but I felt attending a Korean church would be a better fit for me and my family. I was hungry for God and desired something more. I longed to deeply study and comprehend the Bible. I found this Korean Bible study group to be really nice and they were sincere in their studies. A little later I found out they went to church on Saturday. So we started going to a Seventh Day Adventist church that I had never heard of before. Since they also had a Korean church, I hoped my family would also attend and get to know more people. (Some years later we decided that this church was not for us). Mom had never had a chance to go to church during the years she lived in Korea except occasionally following a friend to the Catholic Church and now she was also eager to go to church to learn more about the Bible.

Meanwhile after completing his mandatory military service in Korea, Heung-Gu finally left Korea for the United States. He hadn't acquired any particular skills though, so we weren't able to place him in a position or find him a job. Because he had nothing to do for several months, he grew bored and agitated. Heung-Gu didn't want to work for Bill's company, and the business wasn't hiring either.

One of the Korean pastors from church had another pastor friend in Denver who could possibly help Heung-Gu, so he suggested that I send my brother there to find work. He agreed that a larger city like Denver would provide more opportunities. Heung-Gu had only been in the country for four months and had just learned how to drive, but we got him a car anyway and gave him directions to Denver. I felt awful and was concerned that he was traveling across the country by himself. I soon came to the conclusion that I couldn't make decisions for him, and it was time for me to let go of being responsible for everything. Heung-Gu got in touch three days later to confirm his safe arrival, and we were ecstatic. The Denver pastor

141

assisted Heung-Gu in locating employment at a denture-making company. One by one, my family joined Heung-Gu in Denver, since they all wanted to live in a bigger city.

After I moved my family to the United States, Grandma lived in Seoul with my older uncle Jong Seok. Four years later, she passed away. For many years, my father frequently traveled between the United States and Korea. He resided in many different cities, including New York, Guam, Hawaii, and Alaska. Whenever Dad would need something he would always travel to Denver and stay with my brothers, sister and mom. Dad passed away at 80 years old in Alaska, where he shared a home with his new younger Korean wife. A few years later, Bill and I visited Anchorage, where we discovered the gravestone with my father's name Chong Man Yi on it at Anchorage City cemetery. I had explained the Gospel to him over the phone numerous times, and the last time we spoke, he appeared to understand. I would like to believe that he is in heaven. Mom was entirely different. She never stopped giving thanks to God or praying till the day of her passing, and I am certain she is in heaven. Mom passed away at the age of 97 in Phoenix at the home of her youngest child (my sister Song-Hee).

Chapter 14

Dear Dad

Dear Dad,

Even though you have been gone for many years, I feel compelled to write to you now for my own peace of mind. As the oldest child, I believe I have an obligation to record my life story for my children and siblings, as well as the story of our Yi family. The majority of my earliest memories center around your behavior and how it affected our lives. I have had an incredibly hard time understanding your life decisions, but I forgave you a long time ago and no longer carry anger.

It seemed like almost every night you were home, you would get drunk and enraged after losing money through your gambling. You would blame Mom and us for your troubles. I felt you were a coward by abusing the people you should have loved and defended the most. As an adult, I can better comprehend the reasons you were frustrated.

However, I realize now that you also took care of me in several good and appropriate ways. It's important for me to keep this in mind. When I was younger, I often thought you were the worst father ever. When I was a teenager, if you returned home angry and drunk, everyone had to run from you. I was the only one who never stopped keeping an eye out for you. I offered you food, water, shoulder massages in an effort to calm you down and to help you get to sleep quickly to protect Mom. You never took advantage of me in a wrong way as I have heard other women experienced from their own fathers.

I also recall the time during the Korean War when you fled from the war and went to live with Mom's brother. I was riding on the back of your bicycle when I was about six years old and you were having a terrible time navigating the treacherous mountain valley route. We frequently fell into large ditches, and once we became stranded there with injuries that left us exhausted, hungry, and thirsty. I don't recall what we ate or how long we were confined there, but you brought me some water from a nearby creek and gave me something to eat. I think we ate raw sweet potatoes you had been carrying. As you struggled to escape the deep ditch with your bike, you appeared desperate and were mumbling and swearing. Somehow we got out of there. I was very afraid of you but never asked anything that would enrage you. So I just quietly followed behind you. Later, as I grew older, I frequently thought about that incident, and how tough it must have been for you to go with me yet you didn't leave me to perish there. I'm not sure how we managed to make it through that dreadful voyage. I appreciate you not leaving me to die alone. Thank you for that, Dad. I know you must have cared and loved me more than I realized at the time.
Love,
Your Daughter Chong Su

Chapter 15
Family

After completing my high school education, I continued on to Kellogg Community College and enrolled in English 101 and administrative assistant training. Speaking and writing English was always my biggest problem, even much later in cosmetology school. When I look back, I think I felt compelled to keep trying to better myself after coming to America. Maybe it was because I was insecure about my lack of education in Korea. I learned how to ski, swim, and play tennis. I discovered that I was talented in sports and art, like my brothers. I was selected for the Women's tennis league travel squad, playing first singles. With my tennis coach's encouragement, I developed this natural gift. Later we moved to Oakbrook, Illinois, and I started taking golf lessons at Medina Country Club. I enjoyed both sports for many years. When we moved to Arizona, I frequently won the women's club golf tournaments in Stone Canyon and Saddle Brook. We enjoyed country clubs, especially their tennis and golf tournaments. Thanks to Bill's successful career, we were able to purchase beautiful homes in several different cities where we put a lot of effort into each one and even built some of them. Bill and I did our best to provide the girls with a solid education and to support their aspirations through music, swimming, and tennis lessons.

Bill and I were fortunate to spend 20 years post-retirement in Tucson, Arizona. Even in the midst of all this we were involved with many different Bible studies and mission groups like Opportunity International, and the local Tucson Gospel Rescue Mission organization. No matter how busy I was, I still hungered for God and wanted to study the Bible. Even though I was a believer in the Bible, I still never felt I had a chance to study the Bible deeply. While living in Oak Brook, I completed a reform theology course through a Korean video series. This required two years of intensive study. While in Tucson, I studied an online course with the International School of Ministry. I also studied with Dr. Thomas Hwang who was a theology professor, pastor and missionary. I used his media series and books, starting with "Origins of Religion." These courses helped satisfy my hunger for God. I now realize what I've truly needed all along was to study the Bible carefully. Finally, I am content with God, and I trust that God's goodness and love will guide me all the days of my life. Amen!

God blessed us with a family of five. Our oldest daughter Moon-Hea (Susan) studied architecture and urban planning at the University of Michigan but currently works in Human Resources for a health tech company in Chicago. Song-Hea (Kim) studied violin since she was three years old and has degrees from University of Michigan and Northwestern for her Master's degree. She currently teaches violin and plays in various groups in Chicago. Yong-Hea (Sarah), our youngest, went to Michigan State for her undergraduate degree, obtained a law degree and works for the environmental control department for the state of Michigan. It is said that children are shadows of their parents. From what I've observed, our three daughters act in similar ways to the two of us. When it comes to correcting their children, sometimes it seems like I'm looking in a mirror at myself, but I can't complain. All three of our daughters are Bible believers, hard-working, responsible, honest, and devoted mothers and wives. Our five handsome grandsons are loving and smart: Josef, Alex, Isaac, Moses and Lucas. Our one and only beautiful granddaughter, Mena, is sassy, smart, and very active in sports. She is special to us. We've enjoyed traveling, camping, and spending time with our cherished grandchildren. We've pushed a lot of swings at many different parks! I think this song and scripture verse depicts my family whenever I see my grandchildren. After all, Jesus is the person we should look up to the most, as we examine his life using the Bible, prayer, and songs of worship.

Jesus loves the little children
All the children of the world
Red and yellow, black and white,
They are precious in his sight
Jesus loves the little children of the world!

"And we know that all things work together for the good of those who love God, to them who are called according to his purpose." (Romans 8:28)

My brothers all ended up going their separate ways and pursued their own individual goals. Seok-Gu trained as a mechanic and has a lovely family with two children and two grandchildren. Jeong-Gu and Tae-Gu had dreams of becoming movie stars, and they achieved this goal, as well as opening Taekwondo schools and starting other businesses. They also have their own children. Jeong-Gu had two boys, and Tae-Gu had two boys and a girl. They produced several films, the first titled "Fatal Revenge" and have prospered while residing in Arizona, California, and Denver, Colorado. My younger sister Song-Hee resides in Phoenix, Arizona with her husband David and has a son and daughter.

Chapter 16
Memories

Despite the fact that it seems like only yesterday, the years have flown by in the blink of an eye. At the time of this writing, I am almost 80 years old. Although my life in the U.S. has been full in many ways, it hasn't always been easy. We were not a perfect family by any means. Bill and I have very different personalities, so we often disagree about each other's viewpoints. I'm sure that a lot of our problems are language-related or from cultural differences. But by God's grace, we have stayed committed to each other and to our children.

Every person's life story has its ups and downs. While I overcame many obstacles, I still made a lot of mistakes along the way. My biggest regret was from a decision I made around the time I turned 35. I watched a news special on how racially mixed Korean children like my own were being treated terribly in Korean orphanages. It gave me such a heartbreaking feeling that I approached Bill about adopting. After much deliberation, he finally agreed and we began the adoption process. Our daughters were eight, six, and three, so we requested a five-year-old Amerasian boy just like our own children. We worked with a social worker to make sure we were prepared. It took about five to six months. We picked him up at the Chicago O'Hare airport. We were taken aback when we met him because he was full Korean and couldn't talk. On our way home to Michigan, a 4-hour drive, I tried speaking with him in Korean. I was shocked because he wasn't able to say one word, only grunting "unng unng." We were not told about his special needs. We named him Timmy, but once again I felt betrayed by my fellow Koreans. How dare they cheat me again. I was extremely upset. We realized it was not his fault, so we kept trying to do our best to love him

We took Timmy to the doctor for a physical check-up because he had a lot of scars and he was still scratching all over his body. He wanted to eat nearly all the time but didn't want to use silverware and would only eat with his hands. He still didn't speak. The doctor said he had the scabies, something we'd never heard of before but our whole family had to be treated. We didn't know what to do with his special needs or mental and physical problems. We engaged in counseling with the case worker and the doctors many times, but there was no improvement. Because Timmy was almost 5 ½ years old, I wanted to take him to kindergarten but the school wouldn't accept him, and told us we'd have to send him to a special school, but there wasn't one available near us. At this time, we lived in the country outside the small city of Marshall, Michigan. Everyone said he just required a lot of love and patience. After much thought, we realized he needed someone who had a lot of extra time to care for him. Unfortunately, we were not capable of meeting his needs. In those days Bill had started traveling for work all over the world. I had our three little ones to take care of on my own. Neither I nor the public schools could physically or emotionally care for him. After a year and a half, we decided it best to transfer our almost 7-year-old adopted Korean son to a different home.

Making this choice felt like a personal failure, since I never would have given up on my own biological child no matter what. I prayed to God numerous times for forgiveness for any selfishness in my heart. I prayed that God would bless Timmy and give him a better and happier life. I know that God loves him wherever he is now. I felt letting Timmy go was the biggest failure in my life. I confess to God for my selfishness and ask for his forgiveness.

As I become older, I frequently consider my grandmother. She was my pillar of support. I will never forget what she did for our family out of her love for me as her first grandchild. I regret not having shown her more appreciation while she was alive. I still feel sad about this and that we caused her a great deal of heartache most of her life. Grandma made many valiant attempts to salvage our family. She became the first Christina in our family. I also wish I had thought more often of my uncle who helped me so much. I was a naive country girl when I came to his house. He trained and taught me everything that I needed to know to obtain a job, which led to my escape from poverty. I should have expressed more gratitude towards my uncle Jong Su.

Many memories of Korea flood my mind as I write about my past now. I recently jumped at the chance to go back to Korea when my friend shared that she'd be going to a prayer mountain. I traveled to the Dura Village Monastery, Prayer Mountain in April 2023, founded by Presbyterian Pastor Kim Jin-Hong. I joined the 10-day fasting-and-prayer program along with a group of 54 Korean adults of all ages from around the world. (I have been reading Pastor Kim's books and listening to his sermons on YouTube for a long time. He is one of my spiritual role models and teachers.) First, they gave all of us a complete physical to check our health before we started the hiking, fasting and exercise program. After we finished, we had another check-up for comparison. I was the oldest in the group, which is not uncommon for me these days. The physical and spiritual experiences we had were incredible. I'm very grateful that I was able to participate in that program.

While I was there, I also wanted to see my childhood home, as well as my former workplaces and my relatives. I still have a couple of aunts and many cousins living in Korea. I visited my father's side of the family, and they were overjoyed to see me. However, I ran out of time to see my mother's side of the family. (It's my plan to return soon to visit them.) All my cousins on both sides are younger than I am. They were young children when I left Korea in 1971. Now we are all much older and grandparents ourselves. We had a lot to share and were happy to see one another again. I spent a few nights with my uncle Jong-Su's wife, whom I'd lived with when I was 17 years old. Uncle Jong-Su went to heaven a few years ago. Most of my cousins came and visited me at my aunt's house. A couple of my cousins drove my aunt and me to many familiar spots, including the place I used to work, but nothing looked the same to me because the landscape had been completely altered. The picturesque hills, rivers and little mountains from my youth were transformed, now replaced by concrete buildings, tunnels, and roads. When I was a child, everything seemed so huge and far away, but in a car, everything was close together, and looked so small.

We went to my old village to look for the Yi family home but it was gone with all new surroundings. I could not even find the right spot for my old home. I stood there for a little while and thought about my past. I wished I could find an older person from that era who still lived in the village. My cousin decided we should drive around, and we eventually talked with one middle aged farmer who was walking on the road. I said to him, "I used to live here a long time ago. Where is everybody?" He told me that nowadays even farmers don't want their children to become farmers like their parents or grandparents. There aren't many girls who want to marry a farmer, even young good-looking men, so they usually leave for city life. I felt sad hearing that and realized why the rural areas seemed abandoned and desolate. Often, it's only old people who stay behind. Just before we left, my aunt told me that one of the elderly lady's distant relatives I knew while growing up still lived in this village. She was now 92, the same age as my aunt. We decided to go find her house. When she heard my name, she was delighted to see me and called my name Chong-Hee several times. She touched me tenderly, and we all cried together. Now that I think about that trip, all I did was cry with everyone I saw.   As   I was traveling to my hometown, I had many memories of my mother, usually carrying a baby on her back. One poignant memory was when she visited me in Seoul, her first trip to a big city. I met her at the train station, and she was still carrying my 3-year old sister Song-Hee on her back. She looked very nervous and scared until she saw me waiting for her. My mother's last trip to Korea with me was when she was 78 years old. It's incredible to me that I am now the same age as my mother, traveling alone in Korea. When Mom last traveled with me she held my hand and trailed me everywhere. I couldn't even use the restroom by myself; she was like my shadow. Although she was overjoyed to see her siblings, she was also extremely worried that she would get lost and left behind in Korea.

As I get closer to 80, I cannot help thinking of my mom and her life. She lived a long life until 97 years of age. As she got older, she gradually started losing her memory but she always remembered her family and was happy to see everyone. Every time she saw us she never complained about anything. She was still able to take care of her personal needs, like going to the bathroom and brushing her teeth until a couple of months before she went to heaven. She lived with her youngest baby (my only sister) in Phoenix, Arizona, for 14 years. She loved everything about America. She also loved God, reading the Bible, and singing hymns right until her last breath. She was extremely thankful for Bill. Whenever she saw him, she would clap her hands and say "happy, happy, happy." She'd often thank him for bringing her to America. She considered Bill to be her rescuer, and a very kind and godly man.

Chapter 17
Looking Back

When I think back on the years, I feel an immense mixture of gratitude, relief and awe for being alive and being able to write this narrative.

> *Come to me, all who labor and are heavy laden, and I will give you rest. Take my yoke upon you, and learn of me, for I am meek and lowly in heart, and you will find rest for your souls. (Matthew 11:28)*

This Bible verse touches my heart and reminds me, "Why are you still not   letting go and completely trusting God for everything in your life?" It's easy to think I'm in control of my own plans, but then I remember how many times I've been surprised. Looking back, I believe that God has done this all for me. Sometimes I was surprised in very humorous ways. Yes, God did give me some very funny experiences that I can't even explain in this book. But I just had to accept them, be happy, just like my mom was, and stay humble and thankful. I learned the hard way, but we can never beat God.

My descendants, our grandchildren and my siblings' children, come from all different nations in the world. It seemed to happen so quickly that I scarcely had the power to change anything. The change occurred within one generation after I came to America and brought my entire family to the U.S. I used to hear that the United States was a melting pot, but I didn't think much about it at the time. However, now my family is truly an example of America's reputation as a melting pot.

I want to ask God this, "Where will You lead me next and what new thing will You surprise me with? From the start of my life, I've been just like a little frog in a well, and you've faithfully led me to a very big ocean." As I write these memoirs now, I sense that significant changes are ahead of me once again.

O ye of little faith, why are you so afraid? (Matthew 8:26)

Over the last four years, Bill and I have spent six months living in West Olive, Michigan during the summer, and six months living in Lindale, Texas during the winter, the home of JAMA (Jesus Awakening Movement of America) founded by Professor John C. Kim. When I first heard Dr Kim's lecture after I read his book called "Why Me?" I was moved. This was the first time I had heard of a Korean man who wanted to awaken and train the future generations within the Korean American community. I never imagined that I would want to, or even be able to convince Bill to live with me in a Korean community. There were other large Christian ministries like Mercy Ships and YWAM (Youth With a Mission) located close by and as Christians, we were excited to live in this area with many opportunities to volunteer. We enjoy attending the English-Speaking Community Christian Fellowship church nearby. Sometimes I asked the Lord how in the world could this happen to me? At JAMA, we live in a small 2-bedroom duplex next to medical missionary Dr. Soon Ja Choi, the founder of Messenger of Mercy. Seven other residents who want to volunteer like us live in JAMA's Mission Grove Village, a gated community surrounded by acres of big pines, oaks and other trees. The campus has about 150 acres of fields with walking trails, gardens, chickens, bee hives along with dormitories for visitors. We enjoy participating in various activities and have made many wonderful friends. I am extremely thankful to God for allowing me to live such an interesting, joyful life. In my younger years, I had never even considered visiting Texas, let alone living there, but we look forward to getting away for a few months from the cold winter of Michigan. I believe God guided us there because He knew our heart wanted to serve. I remain deeply appreciative of my uncles and aunts, who never allowed me to go without my needs being met when I was a child. It will always serve as a reminder to me of the value of giving and supporting others in need.

When I'm at our home in Michigan during the summer, I like to wake up in the morning and give thanks to God, then get a cup of coffee. Weather permitting, I go outside to my garden where I tend to my plants, flowers, and small trees while conversing with God. The crisp Michigan morning is often enough to make me catch my breath yet still feel happy and grateful. Removing dead leaves and flowers, weeding, and trimming takes a lot of effort. I'm responsible for a few thousand plants and flowers as well as different kinds of trees, each with their own unique beauty and special needs. After I've finished the hard work in my garden, I feel grateful I can still move around freely. I truly enjoy helping my plants grow with good earth, water, nourishment, and close attention - my lovely flowers and my favorite hydrangeas. (Sometimes I recall running in the rice paddies as a young girl, terrified of the frogs and snakes. I'm glad my garden in Michigan has no snakes, only beautiful flowers.)

I've been pondering how similar our lives are to the flowers in my garden. They emerge to blossom one after the other throughout the summer, proud and pleased to display their beauty and glory. Over time, the flowers wilt and fade away, unable to thrive once their season is over. In the fall, the trees in my yard drop their leaves, until they are completely bare and naked. How similar we are to the trees and bloom of these flowers as humans get older. While we are young and healthy, we stand straight and tall, proud of our youth and showing off our unique kinds of beauty. Yet without our Creator and Gardener, we are as helpless and hopeless as wilted grass and naked trees. Ultimately, life is filled with much pain and sorrow if we choose not to trust God's promises. Even Buddha said our human lives are a 'Sea of Pain'.

For the flesh is as grass, and all the glory of man as the flower of grass. The grass wilts, and the flower thereof falleth away. But the word of the Lord endureth forever. And this is the word which by the gospel is preached unto you. (1 Peter 1:24-25)

As for man, his days are as grass: as a flower of the field, so he flourisheth. For the wind passeth over it, and it is gone; and the place thereof shall know it no more. But the mercy of the Lord is from everlasting to everlasting upon them that fear Him , and His righteousness unto children's children. (Psalm 103:15-17)

With Bill, I had the luxury of visiting numerous continents and traveling around the world, including the Mediterranean, Russia, Europe, Africa, Canada, New Zealand, China, Japan and even Tibet. How could I possibly want more? I remember how my father always said that he wanted to live in Seoul and he planned to move there someday. Sadly, his addictions to drinking and gambling hindered him from his desire to move to a big city. He never took our family more than five miles from his original family home. However, after I brought him to America, he traveled with us to many places in this country. He also traveled to Hawaii, Guam and Alaska on his own as well as going back to Korea every year.

I give thanks to God for bringing me all the way to the U.S. My prayer is this, "God, please make me humble and thankful. I give all the thanks and praise to You, Lord!" In Korea, I was a helpless young girl. Although I made numerous blunders along the way, God's grace allowed me to arrive here. I must not take any of my steps for granted. All of it is a result of God's enduring grace toward me. This is one of my favorite Korean gospel songs that has touched my heart and that I like to sing often.

It's all been by God's grace, God's grace,
His amazing endless grace, now I confess
there's nothing in my life that
I could take for granted
It's all because of God's grace, God's grace for me.
Every Moment in my life I have spent
Every step I took couldn't be taken for granted
It's all because of God's loving grace for me.
It's all been by God's grace, God's grace,
Now I confess there's nothing in my life that
I could take for granted
From my childhood I've lived until this day
breathing and dreaming couldn't be
taken for granted
It's all because of God's loving grace for me
Living in this world as God's precious child
singing praises freely worshiping my Lord
Sharing the Gospel couldn't be taken for granted.

"Lord, Your every word is so true. The gift of salvation for everlasting life with You in heaven is freely available to anyone who believes and comes to You in faith. The air we breathe is free to anyone but I realize most things in life are not free. We must not be lazy. The Apostle Paul said if a person won't work, he should not eat. Lord, You blessed me with so much, but You also allowed me to experience a lot of hardships along the way. You are so wise, God! We humans are born stubborn, foolish. We need tough training and hardship in life to find our Creator - Amen!"

The season of my life now is deep into winter, but my heart still feels like spring. The human body is so fascinating. When Grandma Barnes was in her 80's she used to say that she still felt like 16 in her heart. Now I understand what she means! I'm realizing that I'm changing physically and my body cannot respond like it used to, despite my mind's best efforts. One important thing I've learned as I get older is that you can only truly comprehend how it feels to be old when you are old. Every day I have to choose my attitude. So here's my advice to young people. Don't look at an old person with contempt. We understand how you might feel about the elderly because we have already been there. Please don't try to teach us, for we are smarter than you may think. If you want to be a wise person, then be humble. "The fear of the Lord is the beginning of knowledge, but fools despise wisdom and instruction." (Proverbs 1:7) Can we achieve anything good ourselves without God? My emphatic answer is no! Life can be extremely hard because we have no control over our parents or the location of our birth. We have no power to choose our birth day or day of death. However, we have Good News in the Bible and the message of hope in God. If there is no resurrection and no hope in the promises of the Bible, life is reduced to a hoax full of false fantasies. As King Solomon soberly said many years ago, "Utterly meaningless! Everything is meaningless." (Ecclesiastes 1:2) Thankfully, Solomon's words are not the end of the story. Our hope is in Jesus's Good News, the Gospel of heaven.

A time for everything

To everything there is a season, and a time to every purpose under heaven. A time to be born and a time to die; a time to plant and a time to pluck up that which is planted. A time to kill, and a time to heal; a time to break down, and a time to build up; A time to weep, and a time to laugh; a time to mourn, and a time to dance; A time to cast away stones, and a time to gather stones together, a time to embrace, and a time to refrain from embracing; A time to get, and a time to lose; a time to keep, and a time to cast away; A time to rend, and a time to sew; a time to keep silence, and a time to speak; A time to love, an a time to hate; a time of war, and a time of peace.
(Ecclesiastes 3: 1-8)

Chapter 18
House of Yi: Joseon Dynasty

At the start of these memoirs I mentioned my family ancestors, the Yi clan from the Joseon (조선) Dynasty (1392-1910). Now as I look back, I feel my comments are unfinished, so I want to write more about the Yi clan as I understand it. I also believe that to understand today's Korean culture, one needs to know more about the old Joseon first. This is just a personal perspective and view. There are already countless movies and dramas, mostly about fictional love stories during the Joseon period and there will probably be many more produced in the future. As far as I know, the stories of the House of Yi and the Joseon Dynasty have been rich sources of entertainment for a long time. I was also surprised to discover lectures about the history of the Yi clan of Joseon all over the internet and YouTube. So, I had a lot of help from these sources for my research. My desire is to share with my family more of the history of Korea, as I perceive it.

A Korean book titled *Annals of the Joseon Dynasty* can be found at the public library and many bookstores, as well as on

163

the internet and YouTube. This book describes the politics, economy, society, and culture of this era, including even small details like the names of people's pets. This book also records important historical facts that occurred during this period along with pronouncements made by past kings. Some of the details I share here are taken from this book, along with additional information from the internet and movies (한권 으로 읽는 정통 조선왕조 500 년 and 벌거 벗 한구사 TV show).

Korea's history began in Manchuria and the Korean Peninsula. According to some Korean archaeologists, people began living in this region 700,000 years ago before Joseon Korea was three nations. However, I believe this is just a myth because there is no written record of this story. Nobody knows for sure. Korean Bible researchers believe the ancestors of Koreans are descended from a Korean named Dangun, (단군) around 4,000 years ago. In Genesis 10:21-32, he matches the Semite Joktan in the Bible (verse 26). Personally, I've made a choice to believe the Bible's account as I would rather think of our Korean ancestors existing as far back in time as Dangun.

The Joseon Dynasty existed on the Korean peninsula for 518 years from 1392 to 1910. Before the Joseon there were three smaller nations. The first King Yi Seong Gye achieved success by uniting all three nations into one becoming the first king of Joseon. Our ancestor from the Yi dynasty was Prince Hoean (회안대군), named Yi Bang-Gan (이방간), the fourth son of the king Ye Seong Gye and his first wife whose last name was Han. Even within the early years of the Yi Dynasty family, the nobles and those working for the king continually had power struggles. They would dream up conspiracies, which resulted in fights and divisions. A fierce power struggle, referred to as the

Second Strife of princes, occurred around 1400 A.D. between Yi Bang-Won (the king's fifth son) and our ancestor Yi Bang-Gan (the fourth son) in order to determine who would be king. The younger brother won the battle, and he killed everyone that had been against him, including another half-brother and all the government officials to stabilize his power. His older brother, our ancestor, Yi Bang-Gan was sent into exile to live quietly in a remote place called Whong-Ha-do Province at first, then later in the city of Hongju. It is currently called Hongseong, which is close to my hometown.

The nobles established the Joseon Kingdom around Confucian ideology over Shamanism and Buddhism which the Korean people still followed. Buddhism came through China originating out of Hinduism. Slowly Confucianism became more dominant, pushing the Buddhist religion deep into the mountains away from the cities. Maybe that's why most Buddhist temples are located on the mountainside. Today some people still practice in a mixture of all these religions. Korean paganism is a unique culture that was formed after Confucianism was introduced to the Korean Peninsula.

What about Confucianism? Confucius was an ancient Chinese teacher, politician, and philosopher. One of his core teachings emphasized filial piety or showing respect to parents, ancestors and superiors, which heavily influenced Korean culture. Yes, respecting your parents and elders is a very good mandate, but with Joseon it became just an outward show. Those who followed these ideas tried to appear good on the outside but didn't truly care inside. It was all formality and ceremony, a shell with no substance. The culture dictates bowing down and flattering anyone who holds a higher position in society and addressing them with honorific titles such as teacher, professor, boss, or chairman. They can never address them by their given name. Respect has turned into disingenuous "brown nosing" anyone who looks like they have some money or power in society.

The Joseon society system was very structured and complicated. There was a four-level caste system and even the Korean language uses an honorific system that reflects this strict hierarchy. Both the Yangban first class (the nobles) and the Jungan middle class (the witnesses) ruled the country. From what I know, the nobles were generally arrogant and unfair, preying on others using their wealth and power. I am sure that there must have been some fair and honest nobles too, however most accounts were of lazy hypocrites who tried to intimidate everyone around them. The Sangmin or Yangmin third class (the commoners) were the ones who protected and fought for the country. These were the warriors who did all the difficult things instead of the nobles. Farmers and craftsmen were obligated to pay taxes, but the nobles were exempt from taxes. Certain professions were considered unclean by the upper classes including butchers, metal workers, jailkeepers, shoemakers, shamans, prostitutes, magicians, sorcerers, and performers. The Cheonmin (the man of humble birth) were the fourth class (the slaves) owned by nobles; the nobles could buy and sell them. The nobles could own as many slaves as they wanted, and the more they owned, the more they were considered rich and powerful.

During the Joseon dynasty, men treated women as mere objects to be used for themselves. A woman's life was often filled with hardship and suffering, because married women were expected to care and serve her husband's family like she was their servant. Sometimes women didn't even have their own names. However, when evaluating a nation, it must be done in light of that time period and cannot be evaluated by today's standard. I'm just thankful that I wasn't born in that time when women suffered so much and endured countless injustices. Of course, all people go through their own hardships in their particular era and time. During the era of Joseon, many other nations were also ruled by men and oppressed women. I understand that this is still happening in some parts of the world.

During the Joseon era, human rights were unheard of for people, without power, money, or education. They had to endure even if they were falsely accused and treated unfairly. I believe the Joseon Yi Dynasty was a stain on Korean history, led by arrogant noblemen. The corrupt Joseon era had no choice but to fall sooner or later. I've also learned that the double standard of Joseon was based very much on lies. Strangely, these people seem to be the same kind of hypocrites as the Pharisees in the Bible. Regardless of time and place, I guess there are similar evils throughout human history.

The Japanese tried to take over Korea many times, and they eventually occupied Korea for 35 years which was the final straw for the Joseon Dynasty. Japanese colonization was 1910 - 1945. Japan's colonial policy toward Korea was tyrannical and unauthorized. It not only targeted social and economic exploitation but also attempted to destroy Korea. The Japanese Empire also suppressed the spiritual culture through distortion of our national Korean culture. America helped liberate Korea by bombing Hiroshima which helped end World War II.

At the same time World War 11 broke out in Europe after the German army invaded Poland on September 1, 1939. This terrible war ended about six years later in May with the surrender of both German and Japanese officials. Korea was freed from Japan at last. The provisional government was not yet established and because there was still a lot of confusion, the U.S. sent their soldiers to Korea for temporary help. The north side of Korea went to Communist Russia with Kim Ill Sung, and South Korea went with America with Syngman Rhee as the democratic president. Korea has now been divided into two countries for over 70 years and has not yet been able to integrate. Regretfully, the two Koreas are still fighting to this day.

So, the people of the small country of Korea, first lived through the long-suffering Joseon era, and then endured 35 years of Japan's oppressive rule. After that they suffered through the Korean War, and then were divided and broken into two countries, North and South. No wonder why Koreans have a lot of Han and so much resentment. We Koreans have the word 'Han,' but the word does not exist in other countries. It means resentment from continual bitterness, deep sorrow, and unfairness that builds up in one's mind mixed with anger and envy.

Recently, I watched a Korean historical drama called "Mr. Sunshine" set in the Joseon Dynasty from the late 19th century. Supposedly, it is based on a true story about this era. I highly recommend this drama even though it is violent and harsh. After seeing this movie, I had a better understanding of how awful human life was during this time and how truly evil people can be. During the Joseon era, a system which continued through the 1800s, many people lived unfairly under the nobles. If you look at the photos taken by foreigners, the noblemen often rode around in a palanquin. (A palanquin consisted of a large box carried on two horizontal poles by 4-6 bearers.) I once read a joke about the noble man; "A noble would not dog paddle, even if he fell in the deep water!" If we had to live during Joseon, can we imagine how horrible it was for the common people? They could not trust anyone but had to act based on their own circumstances. They all had to live according to their status and had to act accordingly. There was no freedom. However, they needed to keep moving forward somehow, so they did what they could to survive. This is what caused a lot of Han to build up for the Korean people. I personally believe that this history is one reason why many Koreans even today have so much envy and jealousy, constantly fighting and divided. We all have many layers of "Han," since our ancestors were strongly influenced by their grandparents and parents. Koreans still sing many sad songs from the Joseon era. Strangely, it's very popular to sing those sad Han songs (Pansori). They are almost all very sad and dramatic songs, sung with both deep and high voices. Han, cried out from the bottom of one's heart, with a mixture of gestures and stories to the beat of a drum choir with traditional Korean music.

Movies and dramas about the Joseon Dynasty portray a fancy life with beautiful people and luxurious clothes but this is complete fiction as it could not be further from the truth. Corruption was rampant in Joseon where leaders were stereotypical selfish, conceited, and arrogant males. They refused to negotiate with patriots, banned science and persecuted Christians. Therefore, commoners lived under the shackles of discrimination and oppression. A woman was not viewed as a companion to men, but merely as a concubine or slave with no rights. These short descriptions I'm giving seem so insignificant because the real story is so complicated and crude.

Although China and Japan were recognized throughout the world, most people were still unaware of Joseon. It was a country in political struggle with a lot of shamans that served miscellaneous spirits until early American Christian missionaries risked their lives to establish social services like orphanages, schools, and hospitals while awakening people with the Good News message. In 1885, the two early missionaries Horace Grant Underwood with the Presbyterian mission, and Henry G. Appenzeller with the Methodist mission arrived. Mr. Underwood opened a Christian orphanage in Seoul which later became an academy for boys and Mr. Appenzeller was the founder of the first Christian School that become ' Yonsei University'. The Ewha Women's University was founded in1886 by Methodist missionary Mary F. Scranton. Many more American missionaries would follow to establish resources and stayed during the war when Korea was under Japan's control. I truly believe that Korea could not have survived without the help of America and these inspiring evangelists.

Even today, Korean culture reflects a heavy influence from the Joseon Dynasty. For example, people make a fuss by giving unnecessary flattery and it has become a very natural habit of everyday life. Although Koreans also have a lot of compassion, I find that the culture promotes unhealthy competition and jealousy, which make it difficult to unify as one. Koreans often disagree with one another or fight fiercely over small things. It sometimes seems like even the Korean Christian churches argue more than any other groups. I believe this is partially due to our long history of battling to survive. As a result, many people are very emotional, have a short temper and are not very patient. The Korean people also like doing things quickly and always appear to be in a hurry. Since I am Korean, I too have some of these same characteristics that I need God's help with.

On the other hand, both the culture and laws in America were originally founded on the principle of telling the truth. That doesn't mean America is automatically better; we also have many serious problems to solve. I realize that there aren't completely moral people anywhere in the world, including America. I don't want to be judgmental towards others, but the Bible does tell us that we are all sinners. No one is perfect except for Jesus Christ. We must not look only at others but start with ourselves by looking at our hearts as Christians - how should we live as believers?

> *"There is no one righteous, not even one; there is no one who understands; there is no one who seeks God. All have turned away, they have together become worthless; there is no one who does good, not even one." (Romans 3:10-12)*

Today when I think of my home country Korea, my emotions often feel conflicted and cold. I remember how badly I was treated by Koreans just like the nobles looked down on the commoners. After I worked on the U.S. military base and married an American man, they treated me like a lower class of person. The truth is I thought I had forgiven them a long time ago so I can't help but be surprised to find myself feeling like this after I started writing about my past life. I still feel like my homeland rejected me when I came to America with just $20. My self-esteem was very low when I first came to the U.S., but I gradually gained more confidence and became more optimistic. Teachers and fellow students in America patiently taught me through my night high school classes. Many other Americans welcomed and helped me and later my seven family members when they came to the U.S. In my opinion, the U.S. is the leading country in the world. It is the biggest-hearted, Bible-valuing nation that has taken in so many orphans and refugees from all over the globe, including Korea. It protects Christianity and sends out the largest number of missionaries. I think I will always live with a huge debt to America. I have had the opportunity to travel to many countries around the world with my husband Bill, and whenever I come back home, I can't help thinking that I love America and still feel it is the best nation in the world. Even though it is far from perfect, there are many good people who serve and fear God and try to live a righteous life. I know that we still have a lot to pray for in this country, but I know that the Lord will protect America, awaken this country, and bring revival. A society or a person that does not value 'INTEGRITY and RESPONSIBILITY' sees everything as wrong, and it doesn't matter how much they know.

> "It is one of the most beautiful compensations of this life that no man can sincerely try to help another without helping himself." Ralph Waldo Emerson

Chapter 19
Mixed Race Marriages

Korea's disdain for international marriages and the resulting mixed-race children from 1960-1980 was severe. Koreans looked down on both the women and their children. The Koreans called these women Yanggarbo (which means Yankee whore), and disregarded them as very low class. But I really had a bad opinion of the Koreans with this attitude. These women quietly lived their own lives and never bothered anyone. Most of them would send money home to support their parents as well as tuition for their brothers' education just like I was doing. As I said before, there were few jobs for people, especially women. Usually, in Korean society you need a connection to get any job. In fact, I heard that is still happening today in many cases. I obtained a job because of my uncle's connection. However, later I found out more about these women's situations. What they were doing was legally sanctioned by both the U.S. and Korean governments. Of course, Koreans always benefited economically from this and any other dealings with the U.S. The Korean government also had to do anything to survive. The government ultimately used even these women to benefit the economy, although the leaders and most Koreans would be too proud to admit this now. Many of these women, like myself, ended up marrying American soldiers and came to the U.S. They brought their Korean relatives to America.

During this era, the entire country of Korea was very poor and experienced hard times. There were many homeless and orphans on nearly every corner in the city. Even in this environment, many Koreans remained strongly prejudiced towards women who entertained U.S. soldiers. They were very jealous of people who worked in the U.S. military. However, I often observed many well-educated men living a life of fraud, corruption and lies. For example, many men, even those with higher level positions, went to bars after work, where Korean prostitutes (Gisaengs) served drinks, appetizers and did whatever the men asked them to do. Some of these men also had secret mistresses yet outwardly projected that they were moral family men. But there was no one who called these men out or said bad things about them. Society just accepted this behavior as normal. I even know some doctors who worked around the U.S. military base that were seeing other women. Yet they were still very arrogant and judgmental of anyone who worked in the U.S. military, which disgusted me. I felt so indignant and angry towards them even now as I write about that time. In my eyes they might have been well-educated, but their behavior was narrow-minded and hypocritical. How dare they look down on those women or me because we decided to marry Americans? We had to live with this unfair stigma and discrimination from Koreans, even after moving to the United States. This discrimination was also passed down to our next generation of mixed race children.

I believe that Korea is a country saved by America and backed by God. He allowed international marriages between Koreans and Americans, and their children were born within God's plan. During this time, Korea was one of the poorest countries in the world and a lot of Korean people wanted to come to America. The United States appeared to be a rich country with plenty of resources. Many of the Korean women who married Americans and came to live in the U.S. also brought both their immediate and extended family members to America, just like I did. Instead of ridiculing those who married Americans, the Korean government and people should have thanked these women for helping their families and country out of poverty. These international marriages contributed to Korea's economy during a very difficult time. Most women sent money to their families back home or spent a lot of money when they visited Korea. The Korean government and the people in Korea would never admit this. They are too proud and ashamed to admit the truth of this history. Instead, they tell each other that Korea will become number one in everything. The South Korean economy is now the 13th in the world. Yes we know that South Korea has come a long way and is very prosperous now, but the culture has to be changed from the inside, not just on the outside.

As I started to write my story, I discovered amazing things about myself and who I really am. It wasn't my intention but somehow, my writing keeps going in different directions and I've ended up here. I must have a lot to say after living over 80 years. I'm almost done in this world so I will not be quiet and will speak my truth even if it isn't always popular.

Before I started writing these memoirs, I thought I was already completely free from my past hurts which occurred in my childhood, like the bullying from teachers as well as the other humiliations from Koreans before I came to America. But I've discovered there was still pain left in my heart. The good news is that I now feel very light and free. I think this process of writing was really necessary and therapeutic for me, even though a long time has passed. I've been a believer in God since I was eight years old, and I've never turned away from Him. I have always been hungry for spiritual truth. Oh God I'm so ashamed, please forgive me, I still have feelings of resentment. I continually confess and pray for your forgiveness for my weakness. I know that only by forgiving the object of your pain can you escape from pain. Today I try to focus on compassion instead of resentment. Thank you Lord for forgiving me again.

Scripture verse in 1 Peter 2:9 describes my journey.

"But you are a chosen generation...that you may proclaim the praises of Him who called you out of darkness into His marvelous light."

"But God demonstrates his own love for us in this: While we were still sinners, Christ died for us." Roman 5:8

This book is a legacy to my beloved family and friends.

Bill & Sue Costa Rica

Family Names

Father's Family

이준주	Jeun-Ju Yi	Grandfather
이종만	Jong-Man Yi	Dad
이종석	Jong-Seok	Younger Brother 1
이종수	Jong-Su	Younger Brother 2
이종애	Jong-Ye	Younger Sister 1
이종림	Jong-Lim	Younger Sister 2

Mother's Family

유성현	Sung-Hyun Yu	Oldest Brother
순현	Sun-Hyun	Mom
유영현	Young-Hyun	Younger Brother
이모	Emo	Younger Sister

My Surviving Siblings

정희	Chong-Hee	My birth name
정수	Chong-Su	My legal name (changed by Dad)
석구	Seok-Gu	Younger Brother 1
흥구	Heung-Gu	Younger Brother 2
정구	Jeong-Gu	Younger Brother 3
태구	Tae-Gu	Younger Brother 4
송희	Song-Hee	Younger Sister

Acknowledgements

I am enormously grateful to God that I could document my trivial, insignificant life story. This book would not have been written without the help of my family and friends. First I'm truly grateful for Bill who is the perfect husband and partner for me, my eternal companion and best friend. We are both stubborn and don't give up easily. Perhaps it is because of our personalities that we still stick together. Bill mostly left me on my own with my writing and didn't get too involved. However, behind the scenes, he filled in everything I lacked.

I also give my sincere thanks to my three daughters, Moon-Hea, Song-Hea, Yong-Hea , and even my granddaughter Mena. They all helped me tell my story, translating my thoughts and correcting my English grammar along the way. Sometimes it didn't go too well - we still had some miscommunication and arguments as they are also strong, opinionated women like me. In the end, after many days and hours, we managed to finish the book. Praise to God!

Finally, my deepest gratitude to Sue Haines who has been a YWAM missionary for 45 years. She helped edit and polish my many drafts. Sue gave me many words of encouragement with an enthusiastic attitude. Sue also introduced me to the publisher Nathan Sewell who is also a retired YWAM missionary. I am very grateful and thankful for their assistance.

God Bless Everyone

Confession

"Have mercy on me, my God, have mercy on me, for in you I take refuge. I will take refuge in the shadow of your wings until the disaster has passed." (Ps 57:1)

"Do not judge, or you too will be judged. For in the same way you judge others, you will be judged, and with the measure you use, it will be measured to you. Why do you look at the speck of sawdust in your brother's eye and pay no attention to the plank in your own eye?" (Matt 7:1-2)

Although many years have passed, I think the discrimination and injustices I experienced in Korea until I was 26 years of age, created deep wounds in my heart. As I was writing my story, I kept reliving that time in my life, and I recalled all the injustices I suffered. I felt my heart slowly filling with sadness then anger started pouring out - the hurt was still inside me. This resentment or the built up "Han" and all my past negative feelings about Korea went into my book. At first it made me feel good to get it all out. However, as days passed, I reread what I wrote and I started to lose this temporary feeling of happiness, even though everything I wrote was true. On the contrary, I found myself feeling really guilty, bad and shameful. I thought I had forgotten about all these things in the past and believed I was completely free from this trauma. Since more than 50 or 60 years have gone by, I couldn't help but be surprised to discover that I still had a lot of pain.

I am calling to You God forgive me and give me peace! Oh Lord, I need Your help, I'm so helpless, stuck in these feelings of resentment and anger without you. Dear God, please forgive me for my stubbornness, arrogance and rebelliousness even in my 80s. Lord, please make me a better person. I wish You would show me an outline for Your story of my life. Writing my own story is just my narrow viewpoint. Compared to you, I know very little. Oh God, thank you for the chance to examine myself closely. Help me, I'm guilty and the same as all other sinners. I confess that I'm obstinate and stubborn. Lord, You know me already. My main weakness is criticizing and judging others based on my impossibly high standards. Many times I forget that I was once a little frog in the small well. Your word told us not to judge anyone. Oh, Jesus my savior, I need your grace desperately.

I honestly confess my sins,
Please forgive me again. Amen!
Amen!!

Made in the USA
Columbia, SC
03 February 2025

52608510R00100